The ENGLISH COUNTRY ROOM

The ENGLISH COUNTRY ROOM

Michael Pick & Fritz von der Schulenburg

Harmony Books/New York

Published in the United States of America by Harmony
Books, a division of Crown Publishers, Inc., 225 Park Avenue
South, New York, New York 10003
Originally published in Great Britain by George Weidenfeld
and Nicolson Ltd.

HARMONY and colophon are trademarks of Crown
Publishers, Inc.

Manufactured in Italy

Library of Congress Cataloging-in-Publication Data
    Pick, Michael.
        The English country room.

        Includes index.
            1. Interior decoration – England – Themes, motives.
I. Von der Schulenburg, Fritz.   II. Title.
NK2043.A1P5   1988   747´.0942   88-16522
ISBN 0-517-57122-6

10   9   8   7   6   5   4   3   2   1

First American Edition

PICTURE ACKNOWLEDGMENTS
All colour photographs were taken by Fritz von der
Schulenburg. The black and white illustrations come from
the following sources: *The Bedroom and Boudoir* (1878) by M. A.
Broome 142–3; *The Builder* (1880) 74–5, 130–31; Mary Evans
Picture Library 38–9, 54–5, 86–7; *Seats of the Nobility and Gentry in
Great Britain and Wales* (1787) Endpapers; Weidenfeld &
Nicolson Archives 96–7, 114–15. The photographs on pp. 52–3,
80, 128, 129 and 155 are reproduced by kind permission of
Country Homes and Interiors.

TITLE PAGE A sitting room, which without recourse to the
obviously second-hand achieves the well-used and lived-in
appearance so desirable to those who feel they wish to
reflect continuity and a sense of the past in their houses.

Contents

Introduction

The last two decades have witnessed an intense interest in the creation of an English style of interior decoration which conveys a nostalgic and romantic image of the past. Far from being unparalleled in English history, this interest was already tending to swamp all that seemed modern or progressive even some sixty years ago, when Raymond Mortimer and Dorothy Todd wrote *The New Interior Decoration*. Of the representative examples of the new styles illustrated in that book, only the work of the Bloomsburyites Vanessa Bell and Duncan Grant still retains extensive popularity in England, and modernity remains banished to kitchen and bathroom in most houses.

Those who have promoted a fresh image of traditional English decoration are so well described and exposed by the burgeoning design-magazine industry that they need no further discussion. Sir Terence Conran, Oliver Ford, John Fowler, Felix Harbord, David Hicks, Nancy Lancaster, David Mlinaric, John Stefanidis and others are becoming part of twentieth-century folklore; their wonder and delight in what they have fostered are no doubt tempered by sudden violent shocks when they see the misinterpretations of their work.

This book is not primarily concerned with the work of the great decorators, nor even of the mediocre ones; it is a survey of the Englishness of the English style of interior decoration as seen in the countryside, the original source for a myriad of influences and ideas formed by the inner eye and transformed into surroundings that exude the harmony and beauty of their inspiration. These rooms need not be conventionally grand, or unconventionally eccentric, just interesting and representative examples of a genre that has formed the basis for a style considered both elegant and comfortable — not always an easy combination to achieve. The fact that the style is transatlantic in its scope should surprise no-one, but that it was considered chic by the legendary Parisian decorator Madeleine Castaing in the early 1940s gives one cause for reflection; even in her nineties she continues to practise her passion for this style. Similarly, the Italian genius of Renzo Mongiardino has created superb rooms echoing the English style, and with his inimitable panache he has brought a breath of our countryside to Manhattan and other metropolitan settings.

What has inspired this interest, this devotion to so subtle a form of decoration? On the part of the great decorators it is undoubtedly a feeling for history and places, an insight into atmosphere and character, and a felicitous ability to be able to interpret the past to the satisfaction of the client. In the case of John Fowler, John Cornforth's recent book, *The Interpretation of the Past*, reveals Fowler's passion for his own field of endeavour, for passionate feeling is involved here,

The colours and contours of the English countryside are a constant source of inspiration to designers and decorators. What looks appealing in nature may be skilfully adapted to the needs of the textile designer or decorator.

The English country room at its best provides a variety of still-life settings such as this, where apparently mundane objects are cleverly juxtaposed to provide eye-catching points of interest in larger decorative arrangements.

whether it is inspired by a genuine interest, a love of the past created by one's forebears, a desire for status, or fear of not belonging coupled with a need for a sense of continuity. A complex web of explanations must lie behind many decorative schemes. In this book we are most concerned with those schemes which are natural, uncontrived, and as English as the gentle spirit of the English countryside.

The 'English country room' – everyone has their own image of it: perhaps a farmhouse kitchen with home-made scones on the table, or a large, light-silled drawing room with a flowered chintz sofa in front of a crackling log fire. These cosy images are the stock-in-trade for all publications devoted to up-dated nostalgia and blessed with being instantly affordable. We all know the Sunday colour-supplement format of the comfortable room: filled with warm colours and lumpish furniture, it is used, apparently, for the non-stop entertainment of anyone from a bishop to the children's friends, and for events ranging from a raucous drinks party to nursing the dog. This debonair approach is assisted by the collapsing upholstery in somewhat grubby covers (the flowered chintz sofa long past its prime), and the sense of social ease is extended to a jolly lack of colour or pattern co-ordination and to lethal holes in the carpet – 'Careful, that's where Moo broke her ankle last week!' Against a wall, a thickly polished lump of damaged furniture holds bottles and glasses beneath the too-high wall lights, and the heat from the flaming (gas) log fire will speedily fan the heat of alcoholically induced bonhomie to an overhearty familiarity, as hosts and guests squirm to find the semblance of a comfortable bottom-hold on the heap of chintz-fleshed springs termed 'The Sofa'.

Such rooms are rooted in the random forays of the impecunious and arty in the 1960s into the once enormous detritus of Britain's attics. Alas, the cream has been skimmed and the remains are sour. On the walls of the 1980s seeker-after-English-roots (of by no means moderate purse) are the watercolours or other sundry fixtures related to the same school of stunted thought which produced the dully brown furniture lurking in the room but intended for consumption in one of the more remote suburbs around 1890. How sad that, as the taste-seekers move further from the central-London homes of their parents and grand-parents, they are forced to adopt the old native tastes of those released from their dreary terraces. Where did the original owners go to? Probably, on the substantial proceeds of their house sales, to some 'new town' actually situated in the country, there to enjoy a 'Traditional Country Kitchen'.

The picture of the urban English country room is not complete, for adding to the 'Balham Blotchy' school of painting are those cleverly mismatched curtains of instantly recognizable pedigree: Granny's everlasting chintz dining-room curtains of 1959 from Peter Jones, lacking the pelmet because whoever turned the edges used it to replace the piece the sun frazzled – but it hardly shows. The dark side of these factual observations is sad: the owners are so frightened of having any taste of their own that might not seem conventional, that they seize on anything old as having instant value, irrespective of its intrinsic worth. Which is not to say that they do not like the rooms they inhabit in the week, palely reflecting the better versions they hopefully experience during weekends in the country with or without their family. The more affluent version peddled by estate agents and interior design magazines is 'Belgravia Barmy', a form of grand decoration in which flounced, ruched, gathered, braided, tasselled and

pelmeted curtains are tied back over absurdly low windows set in equally low walls. What looks fine in a twelve-foot-high room with floor-length windows in Eaton Square does not work when lopped off and put in a Fulham house. For we all know what the real thing should look like and it does not consist solely of a large off-white sofa, yellow walls and shabby coffee-table. Here, playing safe means playing down, and individuality is so far eschewed as to bring a genuine eccentricity to some most unpromising interiors.

The commercial aspect of the amalgamation of these two looks has resulted in great success for a variety of American decorators, largely based on the East Coast. To the eyes of one nurtured, indeed reared, in the deepest heart of England, the English country-room look, or even style, as practised in America is as representative of England as the World Trade Center in New York. Elsie de Wolfe (Lady Mendl), one of the first of that new twentieth-century breed 'The Interior Decorator', while promoting her own American ideas on comfort and elegance in *The House In Good Taste*, preferred the balance and relative emptiness of French eighteenth-century rooms, a style generally preferred well into the 1960s by both old and new money for their grandest rooms. Since then, the floodgates have opened, and if the redoubtable Lady Mendl were to return today and leaf through the pages of the major American or British decorating journals, she would find herself back at square one.

The truly authentic English country room is unaffected by any pastiche of a style which has evolved in most country houses from a mixture of practicality and individual taste. The authentic style incorporates a sense of the real purpose of the room for its owner, where objects and colour are chosen because they are part of the history of the house or simply because they are actually liked. The snobbery which attaches to much of the present fashion for English-looking interiors and the purchase of English antiques at high prices may very well produce a room in which an English country man or woman feels at home, for such snobbery is not always devoid of a love of the objects bought or the room assembled, even if the desire is for display of money and status. Such was the intention of many of the noble builders of historic English country houses, best illustrated in Ralph Dutton's classic work *The English Country House*, but we are concerned with a look far removed from state rooms. The rooms perceived as English country rooms are generally those embodying well-sprung and generously upholstered furniture, which became popular and widespread as the second half of the nineteenth century

A welcoming fire provides a cosy background for tea in this library.

progressed and is, in particular, associated with the Edwardian era which tamed deep-buttoning. Indeed, the old established firm of Lenygon and Morant carries on producing the same models with their company 'Howard Chairs'. Such furniture began to be slimmed down from around 1890 leading in the 1920s to positive anorexia, but the popular look is undoubtedly the one which was achieved for the Prince of Wales, later George v, at York Cottage, Sandringham, by 'the man from Maples'. The only difference in the rooms of the rich today is the substitution of the well-made non-upholstered furniture with antique pieces or with 'Balham Blotchy' furniture. The Maples 'best' often went in the containers of the sixties and seventies to Germany, the American Mid-West, or onto the bonfire.

Part of the problem faced by those seeking to re-locate the atmosphere and style of an English country room lies in their own experience of such rooms, which may be slight or non-existent outside the pages of a magazine. The dangers of a stagey-looking interior are apparent, yet a bold pastiche of *Rookery Nook* or *Charley's Aunt* sets with elements of humour must be preferable, if it is desired to be firmly rooted in a particular period of time. Some research is necessary into the authentic components of rooms of the period, unless the end result is yet another messy combination of patterns and colours at loggerheads with the equally odd shapes of badly proportioned pieces of furniture. Draping yards of expensive chintz around all available surfaces in profuse quantities is not the answer and those in doubt would do well to obtain videos of the English film classics *The Importance of Being Earnest* and *My Fair Lady*, not simply to examine the furnishings, but also to see how they were used and how they blended with the design and colouring of the clothes worn at the time.

These films, together with the many excellent TV productions set in the past, transcend mere nostalgia. Their designers have thoroughly understood and researched the authentic details that add so much to the creation of atmosphere. The achievements of the late Sir Cecil Beaton are well known, and his former assistant Carl Toms has gone a step further in recent stage productions of Noël Coward's *Blithe Spirit* and Oscar Wilde's *The Importance of Being Earnest* by creating versatile sets in which the construction suggests a great deal, the props add a few necessary details and the characters dominate the setting. Potential and practising decorators may learn much from such economical use of the props, now that real antiques and period accessories are harder than ever to find.

I was born in the English countryside, and the first three decades of my life were largely spent in a house so English that I am now surprised I survived on the very coldest days. There was ice on the inside of the glass, so frozen that it resembled the tracery of dead ferns with the furry coating of an ice-box. Even in summer the air was cool, blowing a North Sea chill across the softly sloping hills to our house in the heart of the Midlands. On a hot summer's day a cloud might pass over the sun and the drop in temperature was instantly felt. Because the house was surrounded on three sides by trees it was never silent, whether absorbed in the whispering flutes of June breezes passing through the leaves or bracing itself against the buffeting October gales. Now that I spend my life in London or beside the sea it is the music of the trees that I miss in my rooms.

In our house the decoration of the rooms was never complete without some tribute to the trees outside and their foliage. In spring, branches of larch, mixed with daffodils and narcissi, scented the air and, in summer, branches of beech were placed with orange blossom, azaleas or roses. June brought the rhododendrons, half a mile of pink and white flowers with trumpet-like heads, which looked rather sinister against their dark, glossy leaves. Chestnut candles, magnolias, lilac and other old-fashioned country-cultivated plants of the last century, or before, were well established in the grounds and park. I realized how special it all was whenever I visited any of the Midlands towns, such as Nottingham, and I also noticed the close affinity between the countryside and the interiors of many houses in the country, irrespective of their size.

Apart from the noises occasioned by the weather, the English countryside of my childhood in the 1950s was virtually still, far from the noise of wheeled traffic. Distant trains whistled through the night and sometimes a far-off aeroplane droned overhead creating an eerie feeling of space and emphasizing the complete emptiness of the dark. On clear, frosty nights the immensity of the heavens was awesome, and the stars seemed near enough to grasp. On moonlit nights we played hide-and-seek among the trees, avoiding the solid phalanx of yew trees to the east and sticking to the oaks and beeches nearer to the house. We were aware of our local history: that a Roman villa had been uncovered a mile or so away, and that King Charles II had supposedly hidden in a tree along the King's Brook, which bounds the park beneath the lake, and actually forms the boundary of the counties of Nottinghamshire and Leicestershire. When the company, White Allom, re-decorated the Hall in 1928, Sir Charles Allom inserted a Charles II bedroom complete with royal portrait over the chimney-piece. Thus, local stories and the countryside were fused into a magical piece of Restoration-period interior decoration within the eighteenth-century house.

On rainy days I lay on a fat cushion in front of the open fire, reading about Robin Hood who had roamed Sherwood Forest hundreds of years previously, but only fifteen miles away. My England was so remote that I could easily relate to E.E.Nesbit's *Railway Children*, and the *William* stories seemed positively modern, and not only because the way of life and homes depicted were utterly alien to me. On reflection, there were more days spent sheltering from the weather than in the whole-hearted enjoyment of the great outdoors, and I realize now that our forms of interior decoration are as much a reflection of our need to escape the ghastliness of British weather, as of anything else.

Even on foggy days, when it was impossible to see beyond the nearest flowerbeds, the weather and countryside permeated the house. The trees would drip moisture in monotonous rhythm, and thick Midland smogs could be alarming – once an orange fog wound around the trees like the tentacles of an octopus. At such times the muffled cough of an ailing sheep or the moo of a distraught cow, as if tormented by unbearable depression in such weather, was as eerie as any thought of the ghosts we knew to haunt various places nearby. It is no wonder that the English concentrate on home decoration, although even then it was largely traditional in flavour.

Most houses had made concessions to modernity in the 1930s with modern bathrooms and at least one other much up-dated room. I begged to be taken to see the flat of some newcomers in the former stables on the estate in about 1960. The 'contemporary' furniture on a black carpet was heavily discussed (as were the 'his' and 'hers' pullovers, unheard of in the country at the time). But there is an implacable sense of resignation which marks the English country style of decoration through the centuries and is best summed up in Edith Olivier's evocative wartime book *Country Moods and Tenses*, the only book on the subject of the English and their land to convey more than adequately the mystery and complexity of the quiet English passion for their countryside and to explain, almost unwittingly, how this is transformed into interior decoration.

House and Grounds

City houses and apartments lack one essential ingredient for the authentic re-creation of an English country room: a view, which can be related to the type and scale of the room, and which also contains the infinite variety of soft light and colour found in the English countryside. Most attempts to re-create an authentic English country room in city settings are a failure; indeed, a pastiche might be most

A lichen-smudged red-brick church and steeple rise as naturally from the English landscape as the surrounding clumps of trees. The window, linking the exterior with the interior, frames the view with a geometric precision.

successful in imparting a flavour of a true country setting, because it only hints at its intent and does not strike a false note by deception. In the English countryside it is unusual to come across a pleasantly relaxing and harmoniously decorated room that does not somehow reflect the nature of the view from the window and the landscape beyond, whether intentionally or not. The use of musical metaphors is apt, as well-decorated rooms should relate to their surroundings, owner, and contents in a measured, balanced way, conveying a distinct impression of the owner's character and tastes. Harmony must prevail.

Previous generations had a more direct approach to decoration. An undraped view illustrated above reveals a conventional English scene: the soft, hazy image of a lichen-encrusted brick-built church and spire. The thick walls of the room are covered with white-painted wooden panelling to form a deep recess before the fat early eighteenth-century glazing-bars of the casement window, which intersect the view in the manner of an old-fashioned artists' viewing-frame. Clearly the view is not an appendage: it is an integral part of the room's decoration, and the eye is led away from the interior

decoration directly outwards. When this room was first used and fitted up, the contents would have reflected simple forms relying upon the wooden floor as a backdrop to set off the few coloured fabrics involved. The subtle and highly varied palette of greens occurring in English nature are as visible today as they ever were, forming a beautifully framed, living picture in the wall, as intended.

A sympathetic modern treatment of an equally tranquil scene can easily be achieved with the less formal windows of a smaller house or cottage, as pictured here (left). Again, a lush summer landscape enfolds the sleepy village with its ancient stone church and tower. This room is appropriately simple, with soothing light tones and a tiny geometric pattern to both curtains and wallpaper, while a mirror bordered with decorated glass adds a sharp sparkle to the room. If anything, the room is slightly too urban in its very muted treatment of colours. Visually this will be a chilly room to inhabit in winter when the trees are stripped of leaves, and frost covers the ground. It is not a room to associate with the thought of muddy, waterlogged fields, dirty boots, and dogs shaking off water. Perhaps because of that, the element of make-believe is pleasant, presenting a study in contrasts between the decoration — soothing and cool as though overlooking a blue sea sparkling in glaring sunlight — and a virtual caricature of a 'Come to Britain' poster-landscape. Furthermore, as a bedroom with the curtains shut against the deep night sky, it will be an immediate passport to dreams of far-away places, a well-known British antidote to sunless wintry weather.

One of the most successful rooms I ever saw in an English country house reflected this escapist feeling. It was a French Art Deco sitting room, bought in Paris in 1928 and installed in a north-facing room with views of a heavily wooded park. It expressed the same idea of escape both from the immediate surroundings (so very appropriate and necessary in many urban dwellings) and from the frequently wet British weather. Two vast windows could be covered by horsehair roller-blinds decorated with light-orange- and straw-coloured horizontal stripes. Concealed lighting between them and the thickly gathered gauze curtains, drawn over the window recesses, created the effect of permanent sunshine in a room which was fitted with decorated mirrors on the ceiling, the doors and some of the walls, and fitted with sleek Ruhlmann furniture. Essentially a private room, it could only work successfully in a large country house like this, which offered other conventionally decorated rooms for guests; it would

Another typically English rural view makes an interesting contrast with the elegant decoration of this room.

have been too bizarre to afford comfortable continual use as the major sitting room of an old country mansion.

Respect for the surroundings of the house is as important as respect for its exterior aspect if the decoration is to be completely successful. Where a building is inherently beautiful, most of the decoration should fall naturally into shape, unless the owner has *outré* ideas, but if the exterior is unwelcomingly ugly the decorator, professional or amateur, has to try even harder with the interior, an extreme example being the rooms devised by Syrie Maugham and Stephen Tennant at Wilsford Manor, recently sold with extravagant publicity. In the city, where so much is ugly and extra ugliness is not too noticeable, this is an easier task; but in the country it seems as though an ugly house carries the defects through to the interior, infecting the atmosphere and drowning all rescuers approaching with assistance. Even if the house is not haunted, like the Borley Rectory, moving is the best solution, because a country dwelling with a bad atmosphere is hard to cure and is infectious to those living within for long periods. It is inadvisable to buy such a property in the hope of beautifying it inexpensively. The cost may sometimes be worth it, but if

A sheet of water reflecting the ever-changing moods and colour of the sky above create an endlessly fascinating view from this simple hall. The decoration is not a distraction from the natural elements, and blends sympathetically with both the exterior and interior of the house.

The soft colours of an English spring set against the square stone building of an ancient church. Such an outlook can be incorporated into a variety of decorative and architectural styles, not necessarily of historic origin.

it is an old house with a distinct atmosphere, this will linger on in a deadening manner and affect the guests, even if the owners themselves only dimly perceive it. As an extreme example, I can cite my own experience of Newstead Abbey, now owned by the city of Nottingham but linked by common ownership in the past to my former home. The ancestral seat of Lord Byron's family, built upon a dispossessed monastic foundation, it exuded such a strongly unwelcoming aura that I was unable to get past the hall and had to rush out. England provides plenty of such examples.

The potentially ugly entrance to a small but cosy country retreat, illustrated opposite, is a case of the successful treatment of an area full of defects. Neck-breakingly steep stairs lack a rail where most needed on the outer edge of the lowest flight, and a ceiling of boards with exposed rafters hangs over the arched doorway framing an expanse of rough gravel, soft grass, and that prize of all house owners, a sheet of water. All the ugly angles of this corner of the interior are ironed out, vanishing under white paint, and the draught-excluding curtains are kept to a neutral shade, so that landscape and interior are in harmony. That great English eccentric (and knowledgeable house-

Leaded lights, half-timbering and a protruding casement window beneath a pitched gable – as proudly English in their oaken strength as the Elizabethan fleet.

improver), Sir George Sitwell, maintained that a sheet of water was an important asset for a garden; and here the landscape is treated as a domestic garden, so that the reflection of high summer skies in the lake will illuminate the interior of the house with splashes of light, as will winter's brilliant white snow flakes falling to its leaden winter depths. The seasons will continually re-decorate the interior of the house, pleasingly changing all the decorative effects contrived by the owner.

The changing seasons probably form an integral part of most people's image of the English countryside, and the interiors which are seen as typifying the English country room are as affected in their own way by external changes as the inhabitants are. Generally, the accepted image of the country room is a traditional one which excludes the modern aspect in either the house or the furniture; it is a romantic, nostalgic view, not devoid of good English snobbery about our own image of ourselves.

If we were standing at a window looking onto a large expanse of well-trimmed lawn, possessing several flowering fruit trees, herbaceous borders, and a caricature of an English church forming the backdrop, what sort of room should we be standing in? Sadly a tiny percentage of the population would instinctively opt for one redolent of up-to-the-minute late twentieth-century taste. Must this include a plate-glass window with venetian blinds, a polished stone or wooden floor with carpets and chromed steel and bentwood furniture, so suggestive of the institutional to English minds?

The example set by the Bauhaus, Le Corbusier and others in the 1920s only had a small impact on popular taste in England before the last World War, and the Modern Movement, as this style became known here, had little impact in practice until local government fostered its bastardized forms during the 1950s and 1960s with such appalling results.

Yet some English country houses of the Modern Movement school of the 1930s are outstandingly successful, notably those by Patrick Gwynne and Raymond McGrath. They, their contemporaries and many successors have contributed to an idiom as successful and English as that promoted by the Habitat shops of Sir Terence Conran, yet few automatically choose it as a style for their ideal country rooms, except for relatively inexpensive or temporary settings. Nevertheless, such architecture and decoration can fit very well into the English landscape, when cleverly adapted to the character of the surrounding countryside and to that of the owners; they could become as much a part of the cultural psyche as 'Greensleeves', and just as timeless.

But the phenomenon of English twentieth-century life is that for

the first time in centuries the English have all but rejected new foreign ideas in architecture and decoration and have re-created their own idiom. To do this, they have drawn heavily on English styles of the past, such as the neo-Palladian ideas of the eighteenth century, or the brick-building principles of the late seventeenth and early eighteenth centuries, while also incorporating the latest technological advances in household equipment and gadgetry. The number of English country homes and rooms constructed solely to represent twentieth-century architectural innovations is indeed small, while that based on traditional forms is enormous.

The pattern of current English preferences for traditional styles in both architecture and decoration was set in the latter decades of the last century by architects and designers responding to their clients' needs. When early nineteenth-century interest in the Gothic and Greek revivals waned, giving way to mediocre representations, or even gross violations, of the spirit of continental baroque or rococo (especially as applied to decorative motifs in furniture and interior design), the latter decades of the nineteenth century saw a renewed interest in English Renaissance architecture, fostered by the Arts and Crafts school of architecture and design. At the same time, the erection of neo-Tudor houses and villas, particularly in the parts of the Home Counties favoured since the coming of the railways by rich city commuters, led to the 'Stockbroker Tudor' style so mercilessly inflicted on whole communities for the next seventy years or so.

That version of an English style once resolutely promoted by furniture manufacturers and shop-keepers as 'Tudor' or 'Jacobean' seems but a terrible bypass sham when compared with the glory of the authentic English house of the late sixteenth or early seventeenth century, pictured on page 21, yet at the time this non-style was considered an improved architectural form. Our genuine example is typical of the period: a magnificent timber construction with protruding leaded bay windows, as proud as any oaken ship sailing to fight the Armada, and a tiled, pitched roof holding back the weather. This house is as beautiful outside as it can ever be within, and the precisely scaled rooms will always be more full of character and atmosphere in themselves than can ever be achieved by varied decorative effects. Such a house demands the respect of muted decoration and should receive it, or its strong character will crush the owner's efforts to create a restful interior.

Similarly, this picturesque old farmhouse (left and opposite), protected by the woods and hills from autumn gales and winter storms, is an ideal candidate for 'The Most English-Looking House' competition. It is washed pink and surrounded by lush green pastures,

The exterior of the house seen in the next illustration. Soft colours blend with the thick thatch and flagstones framing the body of the building.

An idyllic English landscape, encompassing a mass of trees on the horizon, lines of hedges dividing the fields into irregular patterns, a stretch of water and a rambling building which has evolved over several centuries.

wild flowers, and water; up the walls grow rambler roses; and hollyhocks shoot out of the ground. The small rooms of a house like this would have to be handled with caution, requiring careful planning, for they cannot be in heavy competition with the surroundings, nor so drab as to appear nondescript.

For most of the year England endures some form of unpleasant weather. It seems more endurable in the countryside, however, as there is always something different to be seen or heard, something to be done. Undeniably, the manifestations of the changing seasons are the most enjoyable. Spring, with its wild flowers and buds in the trees hinting of new leaves, brings the birds to life; wintery rooms begin to breathe in the soft damp air and exhale old wood-smoke. The greyest

A decorative expanse of water reflects the clearing skies and flowers of an English spring, and the informal curves of the banks soften the austere lines of the stone house in the background.

of stone buildings softens against the melting skies with barely a hint of winter that has left a ghostly presence, and may yet return to haunt the country dweller, recalling those days after Christmas when winter seems eternal. Quite often, winter does suddenly return. On a clear morning when the sun is shining and there is snow around, the bedroom has a brighter brilliance than on an ordinary grey winter morning. There is nothing so exhilarating as an English room on such a day. The colours are bleached on all upholstery and furniture, and the glare is enough to reduce all decoration to the colour of ashes. It is at such times that north-facing rooms receive the light normally enjoyed on moderately sunny days by rooms facing south. One can then immediately appreciate the subtle nature of English light and the skill needed to select colour in English rooms to accommodate all seasons. Our grandest forebears resolved this in the changing of hangings, a habit which did not simply reflect a change in temperature.

The English, and those abroad professing admiration of English country-house decoration, have drawn their inspiration from the casually formal setting of the smaller country house or from the smaller rooms of the larger ones, but not from the lavish state rooms

The blue skies and melting snows of late winter will flood the interior of a house like this with a glistening light that will bleach the most delicate decorative schemes with its intensity.

of, say, Chatsworth or Wilton; they are to be applauded but today rarely, if ever, imitated. The generally admired style is one perfectly suited to the well-proportioned English house of the first half of the eighteenth century, as illustrated on the next page. The long gravelled drive beneath arching avenues of ancient trees betokens established solidity behind shut gates and walls, no matter how ruinous they might be. No columns of enemy troops have traversed such settings since the days of Cromwell, and none from overseas. We shall not encounter battered façades and weed-choked stables, laid waste, like their continental counterparts, by plundering Nazi or Communist soldiery. Only a lack of money will have contributed to such sad neglect, and there will be no horror story of priceless possessions burnt and family members shot, unless it be as a result of feuds or madness. So the English house is generally a solid structure, haunted only by past generations or bad drains.

The atmosphere of the English country room is all important, for, like anything with character, it must be dressed appropriately: it would never do to dress a dowager as a barmaid – or would it? Current tastes may suggest otherwise, yet travesties of dress do not add to the dignity of the wearer any more than inappropriate decoration

LEFT An ancient tree-lined avenue leads to many English country houses and ends in a gravelled sweep outside the entrance.

BELOW A modest eighteenth-century brick house of pleasingly regular shape is enhanced by carefully tended examples of topiary.

improves a room or its owner. Houses with exteriors such as those illustrated here (pp. 26–9) are automatically stamped with an expectation of what lies within. If some highly gifted individual chooses to abandon most accepted rules of decoration in a novel scheme, the result may be sensational, such as the effects achieved in the late 1960s by David Hicks, or in the 1930s by the late Mrs Syrie Maugham. In other hands the result can be alarming, as in the house where on a dark evening the silhouette of the topiary grows ever larger and more menacing, as if about to engulf the room, stifling house and occupants in an atmosphere of unease.

All four houses illustrated here (pp. 26–9) are representative of established country-house favourites. More than the railways, the motorways have made the weekend retreat an established part of metropolitan life, with greater accessibility matching rising values. Traditional forms offer a release valve to pressurized city life, an escape to a fragment of the leisurely way of life embodied in England's supposedly golden Edwardian age. This pastiche was promoted by the monied, and by their architects and decorators, in what Roderick Gradidge aptly terms (in his book of the same name) 'Dream Houses', which provided an extension of grand country-house life to a suburbanized and mainly non-artistic clientele. The extensive popularity of that dream has spread even further, encouraged initially by the propaganda of *Country Life* articles, then by *The Architectural Review*, and now also by books, magazines, colour supplements and films, heavy with nostalgia for the apparent solidity of imperial Britain.

At an early stage in this development the book *Das Englische Haus*

The romantic image of the apparently isolated English house, secreted in some leafy valley and crammed with memorabilia including jettisoned cars or clothes, is regularly exploited by the auction houses and reflected in the ephemeral look of much English country room decoration.

by Hermann Muthesius explained this delight in urban rusticism to a German audience unfamiliar with English domestic architecture of 1860–1900. The Germans were not slow to join in with their own version of the style, which was first seen among the professional and commercial élite as well as among a smattering of aristocratic Anglophiles with English connections, thus giving the whole fashion *Eleganz*. At home this ideal was propagated in the work of Lawrence Weaver and Gertrude Jekyll, the latter often co-operating with the

Soft grey stone is the perfect foil for the large variety of colours to be seen in English gardens throughout the year and provides a rich natural palette for the decorator. The infinite shades of green mixed with samples of a myriad other colours should form essential study-matter for every aspiring decorator.

architect Edwin Lutyens to create her own distinguished form of super-grand cottage gardens, which in their freedom of plan and variety of visual effects seem peculiarly English. The renewed popularity of these designs in Britain and North America (but not in Germany) almost a century later shows how deep a chord they struck in the national character.

The late Sir Cecil Beaton who successfully revived the Edwardian idea of a conservatory as a decorated room or winter garden was

LEFT Here a formal garden setting combines the geometrical effect of the orangery glazing bars and balustrade with the regularly shaped lawns.

BELOW Animals often form a mobile part of English country room decoration, and the cat is a perfect example of the cosy, serene quality that is sought.

himself a quintessential English eclectic in matters of decoration and taste, and was always devoted to floral displays and arrangements, which appear in various photographs of his. His diaries are punctuated with references to flower shops and flower markets across the world, and his own houses in Wiltshire – Ashcombe and then Reddish House – showed his ability to encapsulate grand English taste in a charmingly restrained manner within the limits of his property and income. The changing moods of his designs belong as much to the times which he lived through and helped to shape visually as do Constance Spry's flower arrangements, which are recorded in her books on the subject published in the 1930s and 1950s. Equally influential were Peter Coats' writings on the more technical aspects of garden planting, for he exposed the 'nuts and bolts' of landscape design and reconstruction.

The stone orangery illustrated here (left) represents the pinnacle of a type of English garden design borrowed from French examples in the seventeenth century, where formal gravelled paths were bordered by box and privet and set out in geometric shapes around some central device of a stone or lead ornament. Here, what might have been a feature of such a scheme remains as a hedged area around the stone ornament. Such schemes were also an extension of the room interiors: the geometric decoration within was reflected in the organization of the living plants visible from the windows. The gardens provided a setting for walking around rather than sitting in, and on fine days the orange trees in their tubs would be put out to complete the formal design. These kind of gardens were usually swept away in the later eighteenth century by followers of Capability Brown's school of apparently random, natural planting. A perfect example of the formal variety, and one of the finest, survived at Drayton House, Northamptonshire, until the war, when many gardens were re-used for food production or became wild. Interesting pastiches of formal gardening have enjoyed new popularity, and that by Sir Roy Strong, who freely admits Beaton's influence on his gardening experiments, has recently re-awakened greater enthusiasm for what is a type of outdoor room.

Outdoor rooms, conservatories, or winter gardens sheltered from the wind, yet trapping the maximum sunlight and warmth, are best covered with glass in our most unpredictable of climates. As extensions of rooms treated with conventional methods of floor covering and filled with sub-standard upholstered furniture, they are singularly unappealing, neither belonging to the house nor the garden. A conservatory should be treated as a giant glasshouse for plants, irrespective of the actual scale of the design. Furniture, added to the plants and flowers so essential for any form of conservatory decoration, must be carefully integrated into the design. This is not simply a case of adding an extension of the house as a halfway point to the garden, rather it is the place where the garden enters the house. Of all the rooms of English country dwellings, this is the most demanding for the owner, decorator or designer — more so even than the hall, which we shall examine later.

Although it is quite possible, by adding blinds to the glazed roof or walls of a conservatory, to exclude over-vicious sun-rays or unpleasant days, this will tend to produce a conventional room setting rather than the desired garden interior. Indeed, it is better to paint the glass with a coat of whitewash inside, the old-fashioned way of treating glasshouses; it can always be washed off again. The interior walls and ceiling of a conservatory must be clad by nature; living tendrils should crawl over glazing bars and entwine supports. As a child I was mesmerized by a long glass peach-case set against a twelve-foot-high brick wall, for it actually contained a fruiting vine kept alive through the coldest weather by the coiled, fat cast-iron pipes of a simple heating

A conservatory should reflect both the garden and the interior of the house, yet at the same time express a definite individuality in the type of plants and furniture with which it is decorated.

system. Once a year, the bark was stripped and the vine painted with spirit to encourage fruiting. This great stretch of glasshouse and vine would have made an exciting addition to a house, for it contained something exotic and alive, creating an ambience half in and half out of the real gardens outside.

An example of simple design is depicted here (above) containing furniture most appropriate to the setting and inviting repose over that most English of institutions, a cup of tea. The intimacy of the setting is plainly visible. The garden ends just at the wide double-doors and is

A formal garden like this, bursting with colour and character, and enhanced by sculpture and a pavilion, forms a lively view from the house and extends the decoration of the interior.

laid out so that it can be enjoyed from inside on windy days, even with the door shut. In that event the plants inside are sufficiently interesting to provide the necessary link with the exterior and not seem like an apology for not being in the garden.

Conservatories which depend upon the view from the windows for their decoration, and not mainly upon the interior design and arrangements, need an intimately laid out garden as a view. Some formal arrangement suggesting a large open prospect beyond is ideal for town and country houses alike, because it limits the eye to something personal like the decoration of a room with its intensified

This conservatory is treated less as an area devoted to plants and more as a sun-trap. Robust furniture and a wickerwork sofa emphasize the informal quality of the room.

use of colour, patterns and textures. The confined, gold-fish bowl space of a glazed conservatory can, subconsciously at least, be an unsettling experience, for a glass roof and glass walls create a claustrophobic effect. It is therefore important to minimize the sense of being caged and also to remember that the flags or tiles on the floor add to the already high noise levels in such settings. Even so, sound-dampening mats or rugs of obtrusive size or design are to be avoided as much as possible. The conservatory is the stepping-stone to the great outdoors, a place to walk into with muddy wellingtons for a well-earned break from weeding, or for a smart cocktail before dinner. It

Photographed during the making of a film, this nostalgic picture of Olde England basking in a pre-1914 imperial twilight remains a popular image in the minds of many contemporary decorators.

must be versatile, and designing a conservatory which possesses these varying qualities is the greatest test of the decorator seeking to create an English country room.

What is this room, so desired by the many foreigners who have never experienced it except as an illustration or part of a travelogue? Is it the hotel room in the Cotswolds occupied for a couple of nights, or something seen in some half-anaesthetized great country house awaiting the sounds of a full household? Is it even perhaps the Surrey house full of Colefax and Fowler chintz downstairs and Laura Ashley in the bedrooms, mixed with vaguely antique or 'traditional' furniture? These components are indeed as quintessentially English as Kathleen Ferrier singing folksongs, but do not in themselves create an

English country room, for they do not adequately reflect the sense of melancholy to be found in the most English of such rooms, a melancholy captured so magnificently in English folksongs and poetry and in the living English literary heritage.

My own perceptions of English country rooms are indivisibly bound up with the English way of life as experienced in the changing weather and seasons of the English landscape, which are so beautifully captured in these evocative photographs (left and opposite) of the farmer harvesting with late nineteenth-century machinery and the empty barn awaiting the harvest. As indicated, my childhood and upbringing were heavily influenced by the almost desperately retrospective interest of the late 1930s and war-time period in the beauty of traditional English life. The post-war continuance of this fascination for what had truly been threatened by extinction has in my case extended to the work of and writings of friends or contemporaries, nurtured, as I was, on the *Shell Guides*, *The Saturday Book* or the Pevsner guides, to name the most obvious sources. Yet few foreigners can be aware of this, and the generation born after ours seems to rely mainly upon cinematic and television re-creations of the period for such influences or inspiration. These, too, reflect a prevalence of melancholy nostalgia for an English way of life in the past, let alone the English decoration of rooms.

Our rooms do not have the German sense of practicality, the ordered French elegance, or florid Italian romance. Of course, most possess some elements of foreign influence, due to our ancestors' and our own travels abroad, but we can test the depth of the most obvious re-creations by considering how a man in hunting pink or cricket flannels would look in such a drawing room. At home, or not? If, as the late French socialite and observer, Philippe Julian, so perceptively recognized, old English duchesses often wear baggy old cardigans, cobbled with (dirty) diamond brooches, and eccentric hats in the garden, would such a person appear natural with her secateurs and basket of deadheads in the designer-chintzed rooms of Park Avenue? Not in many. Some years ago when a friend of mine visited Lady Mary Cambridge in her country house, they walked through to the kitchen to make a cup of tea. It was only when the cake-tin was hauled down that his hostess was seen to be wearing short wellies, because in common with many women of a gardening disposition she found them warm and comfortable both in wet soil and on cold draughty flags. Common sense and no pretensions mark the best English characters as well as their rooms, and truly English rooms are an extension of the best traits of the English character and must reflect this by being comfortable, interesting and, yes, in 'Good Taste'.

This venerable barn with its solid oak-beamed construction and chaotically arranged wooden walls echoes much of the serendipity of English country room decoration today.

CHAPTER ONE

The Hall

*'If the hearth forms the heart of the house,
then the hall is the stomach, nourishing the
arriving, departing or transient visitor with
a lasting impression of the house.'*

Of all the rooms in a house, the hall is undoubtedly the most difficult to decorate. Whether the house is large or small, a hall forms the space linking not only the exterior with the interior but also various rooms with each other. If the hearth forms the heart of the house, then the hall is the stomach, nourishing the arriving, departing or transient visitor with a lasting impression of the house. This impression will usually make or break all the decorative effects sought elsewhere in the house, and so it is important to achieve a well-balanced and relaxed form of decoration in the hall, emphasizing the character of the house.

Most of the rooms illustrated here are not taken from the grandest of English houses, but this should not detract from the many possibilities they suggest in the art of blending any manner of decorative forms and patterns into a homogeneous whole. Schemes practised on a large scale can also be adapted to the needs of even the tiniest country hall, if sympathetically handled. This is not a matter of suspending festoon curtains made from unlikely fabrics in unsuitable positions and hoping for the best, because a fixed feature in a room, such as a 1930s curved bay with steel-framed Crittall windows, will not disappear. It will just be highlighted as an absurd contrast and make the low ceilings of the room appear even lower than those of the eighteenth-century drawing room it is supposed to imitate. So, with the hall more than with any other room, the motto should be 'if in doubt leave it out', as less will be more, if the basics are carefully considered.

One of the most successful halls I have ever seen is that at Thoresby Hall, Nottinghamshire, admittedly on the grandest scale, but a successful room in an extraordinary building designed by Anthony Salvin as a replacement for an earlier house. Set amidst The Dukeries, the timbered acres which also encompass the estates of Clumber Park and Welbeck Abbey near Nottingham, Thoresby is the embodiment of the romantic mid-nineteenth-century interest in the English past as a worthy setting for a rich family wishing to project an aristocratic lineage. The 'Jacobethan' style of the house is loosely allied to the designs of nearby Wollaton and Hardwick Hall, for Salvin was an innovative master of the bold pastiche. Like his Harlaxton Manor, Lincolnshire, or Alnwick Castle, Northumberland, the exterior is more than balanced by the effects achieved in the interior.

At Thoresby architectural effects are highlighted. A forbidding entrance door is set in the massive footing of the main tower and leads to an entrance lobby of Stygian gloom, designed before the advent of electric light. Two Egyptian porphyry figures flank the arch of an enclosed stone staircase, giving it an air of mystery and unease; a right-angled turn half-way up leads the visitor on towards a pair of heavy oak doors set in the stonework. The whole effect is of a journey into a stone-clad tomb-like setting, half Victorian 'medieval', half classical 'antique'. The medieval is inspired by Salvin, the Egyptian (antique) by the decorative genius of a member of the family who formerly occupied the house. In the event, it is Salvin who triumphs with an inspiringly bold medieval hall which greets us behind the front doors. The size is stupendous, resembling the set of Nottingham Castle for the Errol Flynn film *The Adventures of Robin Hood* — the legend commemorated in fine carving set in the oak-panelled library. The historic links are maintained from hall to library by a soaring arched stone screen rising up to the oak rafters of the hall. This screen reveals no minstrels' gallery, but evokes the flavour of an Inigo Jones period mansion, with a broad staircase behind it dividing at a landing, where a life-sized equestrian portrait of Charles I is set in the wall. To anyone approaching the stairs in the hall, it appears as though the horse and rider are about to descend the stairs. In this mood of decorative fantasy, it is no surprise to discover a drawing room lined with eighteenth-century French panelling, yet retaining all the appearance of a comfortable mid-nineteenth-century setting for opulent display.

Here, on a large scale, are the effects which should be considered in the decoration of an English country hall: atmosphere, a reference to both the architecture of the building and the local history of the area, the taste and history of the owner's family, and the decoration of the surrounding rooms and staircase. On a small scale, the application of elaborate surprises or whimsy should be avoided and left to town dwellings where strong antidotes to unpromising surroundings are more acceptable for the relief they bring from dreary streets.

When the door opens into a hall, we expect some form of welcome from both owner and surroundings. Ideally, both will complement one another. Here at Luttrellstown Castle, in Ireland, the late Felix Harbord created a de luxe series of rooms for his client Mrs Aileen Plunket. Although most decidedly set in an Anglo-Irish house, Harbord's decoration was quintessentially English, but incorporated enough Anglo-Irish furniture to impart a flavour of the locality. The Gothick architecture is reflected in the porch from which sturdy double-doors lead to the stone-flagged hall, a practical covering for the many damp feet and topcoats which will carry the Irish rain and mud inside. In the manner of such floors in English houses, a dull surface is enlivened by darker crisured stones which form a rhythmic pattern across the floor.

The decoration of this hall is in the time-honoured tradition of using less to convey more. It has a sense of suspended animation, for the colours are either very soft or neutral. During the day the mullioned window casts its light and shadows, adding to the patterns of the floor and illuminating the mirror in its carved rococo frame. Further movement is given to this static scene by the rococo chairs and side-table, which are unobtrusive in the daytime but will become substantial objects by lamplight, when the surrounding walls and ceiling recede due to the neutrality of their colouring and the eye will concentrate on the shapes and recesses of the intricate carving.

A sense of antiquity is impressed upon the visitor's consciousness; a touch of grandeur is imparted, but not overstressed. The furniture is full of playful curves, hinting at more and better delights to follow — as indeed they do.

As a complete contrast to the last picture, we can see here the same principles applied to even the smallest or humblest of entrances, far removed from the splendour of the halls at Thoresby or Luttrellstown, yet still conveying the element of welcome inherent in the original medieval concept of a hall. In this seventeenth-century house rough stone flags pave the floor, and the intention is the same as at Luttrellstown: to resist the seeping penetration of dirt and damp from muddy feet. Homely antiquity is the keynote: a shaggy mat demands immediate use and white-washed walls throw into relief the coarse beams supporting the structure. A simple oak chair of the late eighteenth century emphasizes the very low-key decoration, as does the shelf holding simple china and pottery objects of pleasing shapes. At night a small red-shaded lamp will cast a glowing light upon the whole scene. No tricksy down- or up-lighters with dimmers for special effects are used; the light is a brighter version of the old-fashioned lanterns and is more comfortingly authentic and atmospheric.

Authenticity can mean a lack of comfort to some, and it can heighten an atmosphere they wish to minimize or adapt. Through the shiningly modernized version of this low, broad door can be seen a glimpse of misty, dew-laden grass which merges into the creeping foliage and makes an indelible impression upon those entering or leaving. The proximity of shrubs and trees can be uncomfortable, with sounds of dripping wet leaves on squally days or rustling twigs on dark evenings. The owners have counteracted such impressions by adding a well-polished, new floor which combines with the sunny tones of the walls to create a warm welcome.

The light-coloured walls of this hall again silhouette an interesting assortment of shapes, from the severe picture frames softened by gilt slips, to the barley-twist legs of the antique side-table. The curves of the blue-and-white pot, used as a lamp, hold the eye, and the glow of the lamp within its dark shade focuses attention onto the well-polished table-top and the objects standing on it. A vase of flowers adds a jolly touch, as does the visitors' book with its suggestion of hospitality.

*S*oft, warm colours form a welcoming background for guests and furniture alike and, if neutral tones on plain walls are used, they provide the necessary link between the exterior of the house and the rooms beyond. An antique Dutch leather screen is used to extend this interior wall, giving movement to the square shapes of the solid, carved coffer and complementing the seventeenth-century family portrait in oils. Books and lamps extend the quiet image of antiquity, enlivened by the riotous carving of the open armchair covered in colourful needlework. The somewhat dead feeling created by all these objects in one small space is vanquished by a cottagey assortment of colourful flower-heads pushed into an inlaid box.

Here an arrangement of budding twigs is used to the same effect as in the last picture in what has come to be regarded as a particularly English way of updating or freshening old surroundings. Rush mats are a modern reference to the medieval practice of strewing rough-stone floors with rushes to provide insulation. The idea of disposable floor coverings is as old as man: in medieval England and later, as Erasmus noted during a visit, the rushes housed vermin and household waste. Instead of repeated renewal, intermittent renewal was interspaced with one or two more layers of

fresher rushes thrown on top of the old, with obvious results. The rush carpeting or sisal variants of today owe much to the influence of both John Fowler and David Mlinaric and their achievements in combining an atmosphere of authenticity with a sophisticated twentieth-century standard of country living.

This room reveals much of the influence of Mr Mlinaric's work over the last twenty years or so. The white walls, so popular in the late 1960s, here highlight irregular details such as bumpy corners or crooked door frames. Throwing apparent defects such as these into prominence turns

them into charming assets and unpretentious reminders of the age of a building, and here the simple and rough boards of the door evoke a monastic simplicity. Combining antique country furniture with these surroundings gives the room a sense of peace while a respect for an atmosphere of continuity is expressed by the careful placing of an illuminated Italian painting, which forms the central point of the decoration. Although the rough texture of the floor covering is not to everyone's taste, there can be no doubt of the feeling for age projected by this reassuringly English hall.

Wall surfaces are most important in a hall, as we have seen. Panelling, for centuries a traditional method of insulation and decoration, still forms one of the most satisfactory wall treatments to greet the eye upon entering the house. The geometric division of walls into distinct shapes and sizes creates a soothing effect, in most cases needing very little extra embellishment. Here, the spaces are used to display a portrait of a girl painted around the turn of the last century. The appealing freshness of her appearance is framed by cream-painted walls and arrangements of peonies placed below the picture on either side of an elaborate boulle-inlaid bracket clock. There is something shrine-like in the arrangement of flowers and candlesticks, but the other paintings and upholstered open armchair counteract this impression, and the combination is successful without being disturbing.

The apricot colouring of these walls, framing the coy-looking brute of a dog in a sylvan setting, adds warmth and counteracts the coolness of the flags of stone beneath the white-framed furniture. The rush seating of the Arts and Crafts furniture, based on earlier English examples, is again rustic yet elegant, and the shiny brass of the huntsman's horn enlivens the setting. Pictures of animals and rustic artefacts are always sound decorative elements in the right setting, and even horse-brasses can be made to seem original.

A front door incorporating the undeniable asset of a decorative fanlight or window is a feature to be highlighted in the decoration of a hall. In this instance the upper section of a wide door has a Gothick arched space incorporating glazing bars of delicate shape. The early nineteenth-century atmosphere created by this door is a reminder of houses in Jane Austen novels, and the treatment of it is not dissimilar to those of Regency England. A vast doormat lies on the waxed flagstones, and colour is provided by walls of deep apricot framed by darker bordering bands of paintwork suggesting a cornice. The quality of the delineated space is similar to that achieved in small country houses built mainly in the 1950s and 1960s by Raymond Erith, his pupil Quinlan Terry, and other admirers of the unaffected elegance of the best, small-scale English domestic architecture of the early nineteenth century.

The whimsy of the Gothick revival, as it has been practised by the English, notably from Horace Walpole in the mid-eighteenth century onwards, holds continual charm. It brings the romance of ruined castles, abbeys and cathedrals onto a domestic level. In this hall a stair-rail reminiscent of Chippendale's designs and painted white carries on the Gothick theme begun with the glazed door. The mahogany side-table with open-fret carving provides a linking feature

from the door to the staircase. The arrangement of objects on the table also arouses interest, reflecting the characters of the inhabitants and hinting at their way of life, as do the gardening tools, boots and sticks. Portraits and prints give the feeling of a house lived in for generations, and the solidity of the decoration harmonizes with the sober, book-lined library glimpsed through the door, where lamplight and log-basket suggest the welcome of easy chairs beside a roaring log fire.

It is not always the arrangement of trinkets or works of art which adds to the character of an entrance and excites the imagination. Larger English country houses invariably possessed a boot room; nowadays in smaller houses this is often incorporated into the downstairs cloakroom. Hunting and shooting mementoes, trophies and fading photographs all have their place in such rooms, and quiet order and anticipation are as necessary as in the hall.

This boot room/cloakroom is a model of tidiness; the arrangement of boots, hats and bags forms an interesting display in itself. Everything is kept ready for immediate use – even the hats are brushed free of what is often a grey, dusty crust. A well-proportioned, carved mahogany English chair dating from about 1770 is the central element in the arrangement, with its back almost merging with the velvety green of the wall, while a selection of prints adds colour and interest.

Just as the boot room is symbolic of English country living, so the cultivation and arrangement of flowers is part of the image many people have of English life in general and country life in particular. Grand- or even medium-sized homes may well have a flower room but these days when houses have to accommodate more machinery and guests than ever before, and a larger number of houses are full of town refugees at weekends, the flower room has often been adapted for storage or to hold a freezer. Many flower arrangements are now designed directly on the spot.

In this urban-looking flower room the unflattering angles of the walls do not lend themselves easily to furniture beyond the built-in display cabinet and the centrally placed table. The wired doors of the table draw the eye away from the heavy slab of marble used as a table top. This design is similar to the mid-eighteenth-century breakfast or supper Pembroke tables, which could also have wired lower sections, allowing food storage without animal interference. The way in which this particular table successfully anchors the chandelier visually to the centre of the multi-directional plan of the room is well conceived. Although the mouldings of the room are highlighted in white paint, the overall colour is muted enough to create a pleasant glowing background. Modern graphics, polychrome coloured dishes and a marble surround to the fireplace combine to detract from the room's disadvantages. The 'overdoor' design has been made into a feature by echoing the glazing bars in the table. This interior relies on smartness of appearance rather than on the creation of atmosphere for its effect. There is no blaze in the grate to welcome the guest, nor is any great reference made to the porcelain chandelier with its crazily twisting arms. It is a very bold piece of decoration which in the starkness of its colouring and the elimination of non-essential ornaments breathes independence and originality.

The paring down to essentials, often the feature of the most carefully thought-out and original English decoration is reflected in this evocation of an English country hall in a house in Hamburg, Germany. A great vase of flowers upon a centre table, the open french windows and a vista of columns giving way to gardens suggest England, as does the large, simple hall lantern. The curtain arrangement, a sort of Beatonesque Regency pastiche, gives as light and airy an impression as the black-and-white chequered floor covering.

The simplicity of the room is emphasized by pastel colours and the suggestion of the Arts and Crafts movement in the design of the table. The popularity of emulating English country houses during the Arts and Crafts period of around 1900 was the result of articles in the widely read publication *The Studio* and was reinforced by Hermann Muthesius' book *Das Englische Haus*. In fact, Hamburg has been mildly Anglophile, due to trade links, for nearly three centuries, and eighteenth-century German copies of contemporary English furniture are well known in north Germany. A successful pastiche, this room is another example of the sensible elimination of unnecessary objects.

An English country hall should of course breathe the spirit of the English countryside and is therefore greatly enhanced by a view of the surrounding landscape, as is any room in a country dwelling. There is something quite stirring about the traditional glazing bars of an old sash window, when as here they create neatly framed vignettes of an array of late summer garden colours. The timeless quality of the scene is sharpened by the nature of the objects filling the deep window recess. English rooms often contain an eclectic mixture of styles and objects showing how the impact of other cultures has widened and enriched our own. Here two plaster heads with their allusions to classical antiquity are juxtaposed with a more recent piece of sculpture, a tribute to the art of primitive cultures. The hall is not only the bridge from the house to the countryside but can also be an introduction to the owner's own outlook and perceptions.

The hall of this late eighteenth-century house with its typically restrained staircase of the period and gracefully arched opening fitted with an elegant fanlight is well-proportioned and light. This mood of elegance is accentuated by the musical instruments on display including two harps, one of which decorates the landing at the turn of the mahogany-railed stair. The wooden floor is obviously a more recent addition, yet it provides a warm welcome and blends in well with the pale green walls and white-painted woodwork. An undraped window illuminates the stairwell, displaying the carved fluted decorative pilasters around it during the day, but becoming chilly in appearance at night: authentic re-creations often need some sacrifice.

The authentic touch can sometimes seem contrived to the outsider, and the keyboard instrument on the left with the music flanked by hurricane-shaded candles may be a case in point. But the atmosphere of the past is assuredly enhanced when the candles are lit and the house filled with appropriate music. The nostalgic nature of the decoration is as much a part of the owners' lives as they choose to make it, and indeed can become all-absorbing.

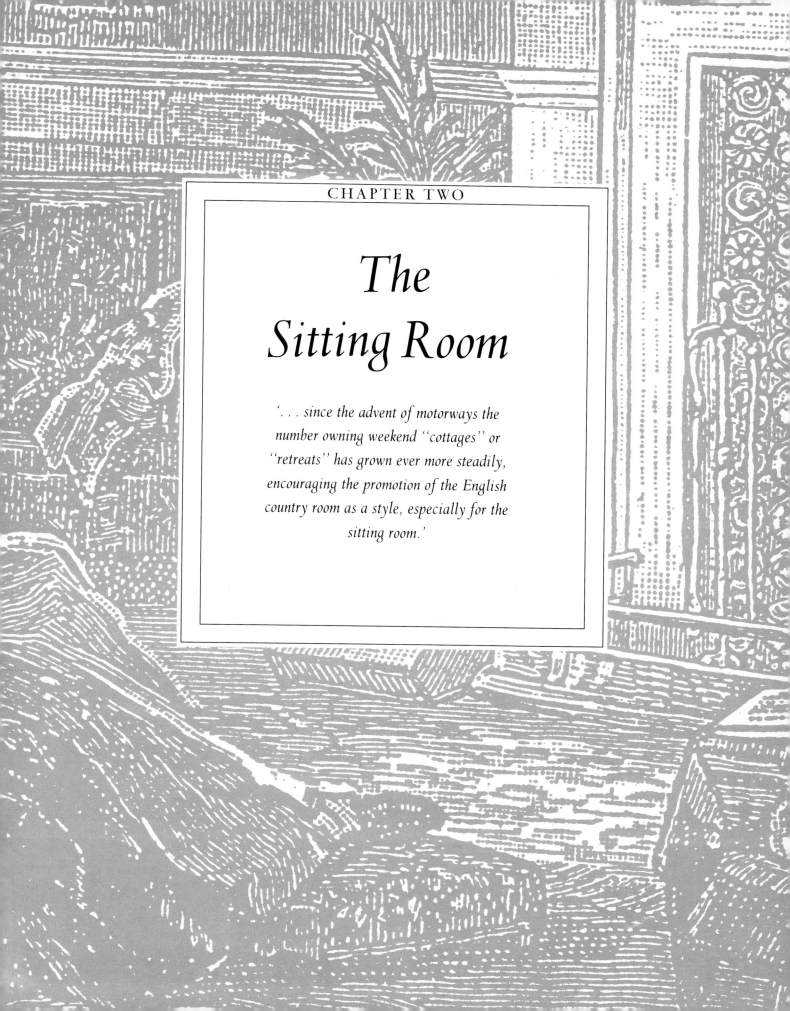

CHAPTER TWO

The Sitting Room

'. . . since the advent of motorways the number owning weekend "cottages" or "retreats" has grown ever more steadily, encouraging the promotion of the English country room as a style, especially for the sitting room.'

The sitting room is where guests in the country usually spend most of their time, and where the owner would often like to spend more time. Only in the larger or grander country houses is it situated on the first floor, requiring the use of the staircase. From the front door the usual connection to the sitting room is through the hall, so, as shown in the previous chapter, the decoration of the hall creates a first important impression. Of course, in some of the smallest converted cottages it is not unusual to enter directly into the sitting room from outside without any hall intervening. Apart from the obvious inconvenience of such an arrangement, there is always an element of shock in walking from, say, a howling gale into a well-furnished tranquil room. But the English country room is often a repository of surprises.

Part of the reason for such surprises, which foreigners or confirmed city dwellers fail to comprehend, lies in the deep-rooted love of the countryside nurtured by those living there. This is often of far greater importance than the secondary consideration of having a highly practical or comfortable house. What might seem comfortable enough to some may, however, spell a singular lack of comfort to the guest doomed to an icy cell with unlined cotton curtains swaying in the draught from the ill-fitting windows. The sagging bed in which the occupant eventually finds a semblance of comfort, only to discover that the sole light-switch is over near the door, is a well-known feature to be shrugged off by indulging in the delight of long country walks followed by huge meals. The sitting room will invite relaxation from these activities with its capacious chairs and sofas near a crackling fire.

In his book, *The Discovery of Europe* (1932), a highly perceptive survey of the various European life-styles he encountered before and after the First World War, the late Paul Cohen-Portheim noted the contradictions in English life still pondered over by visitors to our shores:

The solution of the riddle is, I believe, that the English never live in quite the same age as the other European nations, that makes them seem different; and most of the time they seem to live both in an earlier and, in some respects, in a later one. That is what makes a stay there so alarming to some foreigners and so interesting to others.

English country rooms, and particularly sitting rooms, express this most vividly in their eclectic mixtures of objects and furnishings, and their use of colours and patterns from a variety of sources or periods.

What strikes the reader of Cohen-Portheim's book, is the fact that so little has changed from the early 1930s, a suspended moment of time seemingly far removed from the coming Second World War. If one pauses to reflect on the fact that Cohen-Portheim's experience of

England and his impressions of the English way of life extended to before the First World War, it becomes clear that the inherent conservatism or tendency to be apart is extremely deep-rooted in English life. In discussing the English country home Cohen-Portheim wrote of the Englishman:

He likes a hierarchy, and of course he would like the top place in it, and in that sense he lives in an earlier (and very 'European') age. The proof can, I think, be found in that vast and ever-increasing number of minor country homes, from such as from their size and the grounds and land belonging to them would yet go by the name of château down to cottages (so called): for they are all born of the same spirit. All their owners wish for a life in their own house, their own grounds, as independent as may be of the outside; for all of them country, fresh air, trees, plants, and animals round them represent the ideal state, and you will find an echo of this down to the smallest suburban villa or the most primitive bungalow.

These sentiments have never ceased to be strong in the hearts of the English, and since the advent of motorways the number owning weekend 'cottages' or 'retreats' has grown ever more steadily, encouraging the promotion of the English country room as a style, especially for the sitting room.

Since the avant-garde decorators of the 1920s shook up accepted standards and conventional attitudes to the furnishing and decoration of rooms, there has been a fashion for blending both the ancient and the modern. At first, practised with extreme sophistication, it led the pioneers such as Mrs Syrie Maugham to startling effects. Antique furniture might be stripped and pickled, then placed in the midst of sumptuous upholstery – the one drawing attention to the other. When Syrie Maugham was given the chance of updating Stephen Tennant's Wilsford Manor, the results were extraordinary and the shock-waves have had far-reaching results over the last half a century.

The two photographs here show the same rambling room, where in one part (right) a whole wall is left bare of plaster or paint, so

that the patterns created by the arrangement of the bricks within the framework of black beams are the dominating decorative feature of what is clearly an ancient structure. This is, in turn, uncompromisingly linked to recent fashions in decoration. A boldly patterned rug is placed in the centre of the floor next to a buttoned Victorian chair of the type which became so popular as a decorative device in 'contemporary rooms' of the 1950s. Given a covering with a different geometric pattern, this chair is now placed squarely in the eighties.

The soft pinks of the patterned rug echo the various colours of the bricks, as do the pink covers of the three-piece suite (right), once the ubiquitous hallmark of all British decoration. This particular example has the lines of the modernistic ones produced by Gordon Russell and sold in Heals from about 1938 to the mid-1950s. It has a suggestion of the streamlined look then modish and is unaffectedly cosy, as is the whole room with its huge open fireplace flanked by logs, the oak dresser base and tables draped with cloths. The large pottery lamps have a simplicity that matches the spaciousness of the room, rather like a good updated 'Ideal Home' conversion of 1957. The effect is so English that it is impossible not to imagine the gardens and fields surrounding the house, and the soft colouring of carpet and upholstery fabrics are a constant antidote to whatever bad weather might be blowing across the countryside.

*E*xposing the beams of old buildings is often considered an instant passport to a feeling of antiquity, and has therefore become a popular device. These two views of the same room show how the exposed beams and the stair-rail are linked, delineating the boundaries of decoration in this colourful sitting room. A shiny wood-block floor unites the stairs and hall with the sitting area, which has been turned into a restful island by the addition of the large oriental carpet centred on the fireplace.

The sofa and easy chair, covered in the same fabric as the curtains, are expressions of the English love of multi-coloured chintz. Again, white walls unite a variety of different levels and surfaces on which paintings and objects stand out in sharp relief. A screen cleverly disguises an awkward angle and gives movement and interest to a dull corner. Flowers enliven the setting, which can be judged here with or without lamp-light, as the yellow covering of the screen creates warmth and provides an intimate background to the draped table. Further depth and interest are achieved by illuminating the glazed cabinet holding glass and china objects.

The original purpose of the screen as a draught-excluder is now often superseded by its use as a decorative accessory in the manner seen here in this room, recalling the 'ethnic' touches introduced from India with printed cotton cushions or woven carpets in the mid-1960s and early 1970s. In this room, a shawl is used as a cover for the back of the chesterfield, made comfortable by an array of cushions and counter-balanced by the seven generously mounted prints hung on the wall above.

A leopard skin-covered stool and Regency mahogany-framed and caned bergère chairs near an inlaid Damascus or Indian table create an arty impression, kept in control by the unifying force of the large needlework rug and the glimpse of another room through the open door. The type of objects and their method of display have the cluttered look regarded as English, and have been assembled with a degree of nonchalance that most certainly is English, being neither too contrived nor too ordered.

In this large room, the walls and floor are virtually unadorned, but are so strong in appearance that they need very little decoration, although some must be added if the surroundings are not to appear grimly inhospitable. The rough stone floor has been softened in the centre by the introduction of a circular table standing on a warm-coloured antique needlework carpet. Elsewhere, stout tables and chairs of seventeenth-century design are the perfect furniture for such a room, as the strong shapes of their structures complement the robust nature of the architecture.

With walls and floor such as these, almost any colouring can be applied and these walls lend themselves to the use of tapestries. The light yellow of the sofa and table coverings is highlighted by the urn-shaped yellow table-lamp in the centre of the room and a large and elaborate gilt-framed mirror set between lancet windows. The very austerity of the room is somewhat unusual in England, but is a form of decoration that respects the architecture, suggesting at its most basic an impregnable refuge from the elements.

As a complete contrast to the previous picture, we see here (left) the 'cosy corner' approach to the creation of a quiet English country room, where the emphasis is on bodily comfort and intimacy. The use of neutral mattress-ticking fabric for covering the easy chair is a device first introduced on any scale in the 1950s. It makes a stout cover, and the pattern is also sufficiently muted in design to allow the use of strong colour and patterns elsewhere, as with the lamp and the cushion. The introduction of a marble French chimneypiece is as sophisticated as the decorative use of lilies in a pot on the table, adding a touch of urbanized country living, with a *fin de siècle* flavour.

A similar note to the last picture is struck in the urban form of country living illustrated here (right). A decorative screen is once more used to great effect, but this time it is suspended flat on the wall and lit in the manner of an oil painting. A comfortable corner for bridge parties is arranged in front of a heavily draped window, and large plants are dotted around the room, where the dominating feature is a lavishly fringed and heavily cushioned sofa on an oriental carpet. The neutral colouring of the walls and sofa acts as a foil to the patterns on the table covering and cushions. A large and elaborate chandelier hangs overhead. If nothing in the room appears to go with anything else, this is not treated as a disaster but as a feature. Somehow the whole scheme is so eccentrically English it will work when filled with people bent on entertainment and relaxation. For this is a room constructed for such usage, as the inevitable drinks tray beneath the screen reveals.

*I*n addition to the welcoming blaze of the log fire, everything about this sitting room breathes a peaceful country welcome. The generously shaped wing chair in the corner by the window beckons the guest to read there, and, as the light fades, the considerately positioned lamp will provide the necessary illumination once the curtains have shut out the darkening view. The small table is just big enough to hold a welcome drink and the arrangement of flowers delights the eye. Overhead, a large beam dissects the room and the division is bridged below by a gilt and white bergère chair in the style of

1800, with an extrovert striped covering, which adds a cheery note to an otherwise subdued setting.

Luckily, the owners of this room have not been tempted to overdress the plain windows, and the room benefits from curtains with simple knife-pleats hung from curtain rings on poles. A discreet border has been applied to the edges of the light-coloured curtains so that, when drawn in the evening, only the border and folds of the fabric make an impression. Porcelain, wall lights and an oval, gilt-framed mirror complete the decoration of the wall above the chimneypiece, and the other walls are

hung with pictures. Various flower arrangements are placed on the useful tables around the room, and the oriental carpet in front of the fire blends happily with a low, lacquer, chinoiserie table.

This harmonious assembly of differing styles of furniture is a felicitous example of how an English room may be enlivened by the use of one strikingly different object, in this instance the chair covered with a striped fabric. As one can appreciate, the object must be worthy of such treatment, or made worthy of it, otherwise the effect will be absurdly contrived.

Not all sitting rooms are intended for the entertainment of country friends or visitors, they are often planned primarily as snug retreats in which the owner may peacefully relax, read or listen to music. This room has something of the donnish flavour peculiar to British academics, whether in the ancient universities of Oxford or Cambridge or even further afield. It is a room for contemplation, creation and work.

On the wide, polished wood floorboards are oriental rugs whose bold patterns are tamed by the soft colours of the wool. The ceiling has a dark stain formed by the smoke and heat of the candles in the brass chandelier. The owner clearly appreciates the inherent atmosphere of this old room and has emphasized it by the addition of eighteenth-century mahogany tables and an antique bureau; the 'smoker's chair' is made comfortable by a thick cushion. One armchair is covered in a startling chintz of exotic design, but the main impression of comfort is created by the large sofa in front of the window. Covered in a deep pink fabric, it is a source of distinct colour, compared to which the paintings and curtains appear to be quite muted. The resulting combination of the many patterns and colours with a variety of differing paintings and objects in this one small room is highly personal. It is for this reason that the room is interesting, forming in spite of everything a unified piece of decoration full of character.

*J*ust as the chintz-covered armchair struck a discordant but amusing note in the last sitting room, so this room (above), an extension of a hall, combines a variety of contrasting elements now considered smart by those seeking to create a feeling of traditional country living. The room has the intrinsic merits of an interestingly modelled old stone chimneypiece facing a deep bay window. At the far end are the entrance and hall, lacking a partition wall, as in so many old English houses in the countryside. The nearly obligatory chintz-covered armchair is found immediately on entering, but is drowned in the presence of the two white elephantine sofas that dominate the room. Part of the newish form of decorating English country rooms in a traditional

manner is to overemphasize the main elements and so poke the spectator in the eye. That is the effect of this sitting room when empty of people.

Individually, chairs, tables, fabrics and decoration are of a very high standard. The quality of the curtains is excellent, but there is so much of them – and the pelmets. Similarly, the carpet is beautiful, but the contrast with the curtains is too strong and does not create a relaxed, easy atmosphere in the traditional manner aimed at. Nor is this helped by the addition of even more colours in the abundant flower arrangements. Although a good setting for a large and noisy party, this is not a room which soothes or seduces the viewer as it seems to be trying too hard to make an impression, something the English have never much cared for.

The antithesis of the 1890s-style interior of the previous picture is illustrated by this witty re-creation of the spirit of country rooms past. With the three magnificent portraits the room is already half decorated, and the addition of some well-chosen pieces of antique furniture and objects, interspersed with modern pieces, is well considered.

The carpet is a unifying factor in this deceptively simple arrangement of varying shapes and textures, which shows both an eye for balance and a well-controlled colour sense. The discreet pattern of the carpet is akin to a Roman mosaic floor in the regularity of the small repeated design, and lends itself to a regular arrangement of the furniture: if a vertical line was to be drawn plumb through the middle of this picture, then each half would mirror the other in terms of balanced mass and scale. The neo-Classical idiom suggested by the period of the paintings and furniture is updated by the use of a modern sofa and the lamps on their modern plinths. The light colour of the walls, carpet and upholstery fabrics is an echo of colours favoured at intervals by English decorators from the eighteenth century to the present day, and especially by those seeking a balanced and discreet setting in which a few well-chosen paintings and pieces of antique furniture are a background for elegant entertaining, and where the character of hosts and guests are not overpowered by the surroundings.

This is an English form of decoration which is not unlike some of the best continental and American decoration. The understated use of colours and objects, however, is peculiarly English and the result is more a drawing than a sitting room.

Although this sitting room (above) is more a drawing room in the sense that it is larger and more formal than the term 'sitting room' would suggest, there is a distinctly English flavour to it, even though the house is in the West Indies. It is a star example of the traditional English country sitting or drawing room as envisaged and re-created in various parts of the British empire from about 1900 onwards. The delightful panelling is worthy of Betjeman's Miss Joan Hunter-Dunn's presence, with its suggestion of solid Surrey houses surrounded by foliage and tennis club dances. The beckoning sofas and chairs have the deep-sprung comfort and solid shapes of those sold by the old, established firms of Maples or Waring & Gillow from

around the turn of the century onwards. The beautifully polished floor with a few well-chosen carpets, the hint of a Queen Anne chair in one corner and the pale jade-coloured pottery lamps are as soothing as the pale green walls and white paintwork, formerly smart colouring for thousands of British sitting rooms and no less delightful in tropical climes, where the soothing effect is doubly appreciated.

The triumph of this room lies not in the excellent choice of colour and furnishings, but in the fact that despite its Englishness it does not seem absurd in its location. The open and airy atmosphere created by such decoration is ideal for an informal, outdoor way of life centred on the surrounding landscape.

The 'traditional' is clearly the key-note of this well-known sitting room in a house on the south side of the Thames facing St Paul's. It is included because the owner has captured both the atmosphere of the house and the roots of the style from which the English country room has evolved in its traditional forms, here set within a seventeenth-century town house. A modern wallpaper with a tiny trellis design printed in green is used as the background for an astonishing variety of furniture styles, objects and colours, and this kaleidoscope approach is indeed characteristic of many English interiors. Substance is given to the whole ensemble by the well-filled bookcases lining the walls and the large, open fireplace filling a corner of the room.

It is the unusual position of the fireplace that allows such a variety of furniture to be united in a strangely harmonious manner. The gate-legged, oak table placed in the very centre of the room forms the focal point from which all other furnishings take their position: the chairs near the fire, those against the walls on either side of a writing table, and the Knole sofa – all look towards the centre table with its load of books, flowers and disquieting skull. The room is sombre in tone, and has a strong sense of the past emphasized by the use of candles in the chandelier. Localized lighting is given by modern fittings and candlesticks on the table, and more candlesticks are glimpsed on the oak coffer in the hall. There is little of twentieth-century London in this room, and the only hint at the position of the house is given by the painting of St Paul's Cathedral hanging on the wall near the door. The impression of past centuries is typical of, say, a country rectory in a remote corner of some English shire. It expresses at its best the current passion for the English country room in a city setting.

A continental tribute to the urban English country room is pictured in this Hamburg house, which also contains a pastiche of a Beatonesque hall shown on page 52. There has long existed a north German reverence for English forms of architecture and decoration and this has generally resulted in pleasing buildings with inventive interiors. This entertaining interior has been planned with a great deal of wit, although it lacks some of the practical German elements which made their earlier interiors at the turn of the century an improvement on many English models.

In this pastiche of a drawing room fit for a star of the stage around 1910, the short windows are fabulously overdressed with elaborate pelmets in front of festoon curtains. Floor-length curtains of a voluminous design ('Belgravia Barmy') are lashed to the walls with thick silk ropes and

tassels, which then escape to throttle the necks of the ceramic urns which form the bases of the lamps placed between the three sofas. The curtains if, or whenever, drawn will obliterate the three exposed radiators surely necessary in a north German winter. The fantasy of the sofa covers with their deep fringes is as shocking as their juxtaposition with the curtains and the antique Aubusson-style carpet, added to which is the strong and equally unrelated pattern of the black-and-white flooring continued from the hall. Although these flagstones certainly give a flavour of continuity to the rooms, it is unnecessary in this context, for a fantasy such as this room needs to be separated from the rest of the house. That this is a room for entertainment is made clear by the generous drinks tray on top of the pretty Louis xv commode to the right of the entrance.

Furnishing a room from scratch to create the image of a space inhabited for some considerable time, or with the feeling of old possessions reused, is a skilled art, instinctively present in some people or mastered with varying degrees of success by others. In this room (right) many of the qualities of English country decoration can be seen in the treatment of a constricted corner space between the window and the chimneypiece, which will be affected in different ways by the daylight on one side and the artificial light at night on the other.

The window is framed by faded striped curtains bearing an Empire motif of a laurel wreath; the fringed pelmet above is suspended from a carved giltwood board. In the corner nearest the window a late eighteenth-century mahogany side chair covered in well-used pink repp links the countryside to the interior by means of a cushion embroidered with butterflies and daisies. The effects are not too contrived nor is there too much concern about details, like the cushion being upside down, for this is unimportant in the context of the organization of the objects on the commode and the pictures above it, set against the matt dark olive-green of the walls. The variety of shapes and sizes of the pictures lends itself to an intimate arrangement, creating something akin to a room within a room.

On the late eighteenth-century continental inlaid commode a sympathetic cultural contrast is provided by a collection of Asian art, brought to life by the vase of flowers, again a link with the gardens outside the room. This arrangement does not conflict with the bolder and more obvious decoration of the fireplace, where wall lights flank the large oil painting above, and a variety of smaller objects mount the wall and surround the painting, forming a natural link for the eye to follow. The atmosphere of peace and interest evoked by this natural-looking form of decoration with its beautiful objects and surroundings is characteristic of the most successful English country rooms, for it not only evokes a sense of history, but also quietly seeks to absorb the guest into its atmosphere and hints at the interests and character of the host.

CHAPTER THREE

The Fireplace

'There is nothing so tasty as toast done in front of the fire, chestnuts roasted on the hearth shovel, or cocoa cooked in a saucepan over the fire, with its slight hint of smoke flavouring the brew.'

The open hearth is so much a part of the English country or town room, that we tend to overlook the many roles it plays in the decoration of any room blessed or cursed with such an architectural feature. For a feature it is, whether empty and dead or filled with whatever fancy the owner chooses, should a working fire not be practical. If removed, it retains a ghostly presence in the form of an unmistakable chimney breast protruding into the room – often too far to welcome the positioning of furniture – and creating recesses whose depth is accentuated by their absorption of other more suitable arrangements of furniture.

Since the secret of creating fire was discovered, the English have cherished and developed their open hearths and, while the northern Europeans have for nearly three centuries done exactly the same with neatly placed stoves of porcelain or tiled and metal finishes, the English have clung to the draughty impracticalities of open fires. How much cleaner and snugger such stoves are, and how useful in the arrangement of furnishings within a room! A pipe removes smoke to a handy flue without the necessity of a dominating chimney breast. The decoration can focus upon the furniture of the room without worrying about a semblance of symmetry, usually dictated by the central position of a fireplace in a wall. Yet the English continue to install fireplaces as their ancestors have done for centuries. Part of the reason is the undeniable appeal of crackling logs and dancing firelight, a kind of living spirit forming the heart of the room if not the house. The 'coal effect' electric fire in all its awfulness is, however grand the design, a piece of substitute nonsense, with its chunks of amber glass mixed with real coal above a glass-enclosed framework and lit within by yellow and orange bulbs. The rippling shadow-effect in the 'coals', produced by foil wheels rotating in the heat of the bulbs, is an ingenious device which has been used in many of the grandest hearths, dating back to the Berry Magicoal grates of the 1920s. There is a fascination to such literally transparent fakery not found in the more believable gas log fire; it is reminiscent of the prop for a tense 1940s Barbara Stanwyck movie-scene played in a ceilingless room full of dancing shadows which are flung by regular flames lapping around cast-iron 'logs'. The mini-versions are now found in countless English countrified rooms, and are a distinct improvement on the old Mr Therm gas fire.

As a child and youth, I spent a great deal of time on days when I could not go out lying in front of the fire playing with toys or reading, and the weather was often rotten, even in July, so that fires were usually on the go. For such a static winter activity as reading in front of the fire it was necessary to develop the habits of a piece of meat on a spit and turn the other chilly flank to the fire before the smell of a scorching pullover led to worse.

It was more pleasant after tea time, when the wintery sky was excluded, along with draughts, by drawing the thick curtains with their interlining of woollen blanket. A bolster cushion at the foot of the door excluded the keenest draughts, but allowed in enough air to propel the smoke up the chimney, along with shrinking pieces of glowing carbonated paper. There is nothing so tasty as toast done in front of the fire, chestnuts roasted on the hearth shovel, or cocoa cooked in a saucepan over the fire, with its slight hint of smoke flavouring the brew. There is no logical reason for our unreasoning retention of open fireplaces, except that we like their presence and the effects they create, as much as the dubious heat they provide. But ever since the inhabitants of England waved the Romans farewell over 1500 years ago, and gladly allowed their villas complete with central heating systems to collapse and vanish, the fireplace has remained part of the English room. Robert Adam failed to gain much attention for his revised plans of the Roman achievements in heating, but in the middle of the nineteenth century rich Englishmen began to experiment with steam-heating. It is only since the 1960s and popular extensive travel to hotter climates, such as Spain or Greece, that there has been a mass demand for central heating in English houses, decades behind the rest of Europe. Yet the old-fashioned fireplace is still part of an English house new or old.

The study of a Cambridge don, illustrated left, reveals a corner-sited fireplace that is as demanding of the decorator's talents as if it were centrally positioned. It has been made more of a feature by positioning a Regency convex mirror above it and the usual donnish clutter of invitations and cards beneath, not just on one shelf, but on two. However, this is fully part of the look of this room. A large and very pretty carpet of the 1900s *goût Ritz* style fills the room and is wisely left as the best decorative feature, although somewhat at odds with the leafy-patterned raspberry-toned wallpaper. The owner's wife has found a novel way of warning approaching strangers off the holes in the carpet by simply covering them with copies of *Country Life*.

Such pieces of furniture as the moss-green-covered chesterfield and the art-nouveau brass and wood table at one end add to the undoubted elegance of this unpretentious setting. With a cheerful fire, tea and crumpets, it would be pleasant to spend some hours there, as it would be to use the spacious desk next to the bookcase.

The cosiness of a room with an open fire was often compounded by the addition of wooden panelling, which is just as desirable today if not for the original reason of insulation. Although pine-panelling was meant to be painted, the mellow colouring of stripped, waxed pine forms an attractive background for a variety of furnishings and decorative effects. This Belgravia drawing room is not dominated by the chimneypiece, because it is so clearly a part of the total decorative scheme, the carving at ease with other carved details around the cornice and wide panels.

A feeling for the countryside is reflected by the deep green of the bordered carpet and the lavish swags of dried flowers by Ken Turner. The donkey-coloured sofa covers give greater emphasis to a superb pair of Sheraton period card-tables and a magnificently carved pair of mid-eighteenth-century giltwood mirrors. However, a sterile atmosphere is avoided by the use of living plants and simple arrangements of cut flowers; although the room is countrified, it is neither pastiche nor outright deception. An oil painting over the fireplace depicts Horse Guards Parade at the heart of London, left unframed and thus not in competition with the gilt or carving nearby. This restrained, harmonious method of decoration has developed from the early 1900s, when serious attempts were made to create 'modern' eighteenth-century interiors in a manner such as to enhance the occupants.

The charm of this simple fireplace is undoubted. It exemplifies the appeal of the coal fire for the English, with a snug look which is as countrified as a small house might achieve, whether in the real country or in a Pimlico flat. The well-stocked bookcases are crammed with information to be absorbed, and the reader will be safely ensconced in one of the ancient chairs so temptingly placed by the fire. If the fireplace was filled with a piece of hardboard and fitted with a two-bar electric fire, the result would definitely not be so inviting to English eyes. Yet, as long ago as 1932 our continental Anglophile visitor Mr Cohen-Portheim was writing:

About 1900 English people abroad might be astounded to find no bathroom in quite a wealthy home, or one to be used once a week after due warning had been given; today continental visitors cannot think how the English manage without constant hot running water, central heating and lifts, and a water-jug and basin or a coal fire seem to them strange archaisms.

*A*rchaic a coal fire may have been, yet it was at the heart of most smokey houses until well into the 1960s if not the 1970s. The fact is, it forms as much a part of the traditional English room as that mid-nineteenth-century tradition exported from Germany, the Christmas tree, now so much a feature of English rooms at Christmas that a distinction between town and country is again blurred.

A Christmas tree with real candles flickering dimly in the darkened room illuminated only by the crackling logs in the grate forms my earliest continuing memories of country Christmases past. The faint smell of woodsmoke was overlaid with the scent of singed spruce, fir, or yew-tree from the copses or plantation. As in this room, glass ornaments twinkled brightly in the candle- and fire-light, reflecting intriguingly distorted images of the room with the glow of their artificial colouring. At such times, all forms of decoration are subordinated to flame and fire, the shadows created having more decorative value than anything else in the room, and the normally forgotten ceiling suddenly becoming prominent in the shifting light. The plasterwork grows and moves, shrinks or threatens, while once friendly chairs loom menacingly large, the vanguard of dimly perceived shadowy forms of furniture massed against the walls ready for the onslaught. At such times the dim glow of the illuminated, glass wave-band indicator on the wireless was most reassuring if it was 'Children's Hour' – unless the eerie voice announced 'Journey into Space'! There was also the hope that the extra deep Christmas silence might mean a snowfall.

The extraordinary room depicted here is a positive study in Englishness, again in a manner equally at ease in town or country. The dead-green walls are background to an assembly of objects looking partly like stock from the 'Old Curiosity Shop' and partly like that from a housekeeper's sitting room, with the well-used library-type easy chairs sitting like two defiant old-age pensioners awaiting an overdue visit from 'Meals on Wheels'.

The undoubted value of some of the unused vases and glass on display is at complete variance with the appearance of the chairs, comfortable though they assuredly are. Furthermore, the 1960s 'Habitat' look inherent in the stripped floorboards is also in plain contrast to the festooned chintz curtains, but no-one can deny the welcoming glow of the coal fire in the cast-iron and tiled surround, even if it is devoid of its accustomed chimneypiece. The tin bath full of reading matter is a practical touch in what is a most English exercise in eccentricity, preferable to so many other attempts, because the objects and the colours used are blended into a unified decorative scheme.

The image many will have of the fireplace in an English country room will undoubtedly correspond to the large open hearth of medieval design illustrated here. It is certainly the simplest design and one admirably constructed for burning massive logs in order to heat an equally massive room. The dogs on the rug, the tapestry on the rough stone walls, all convey a timeless image brought up to date by the circular table draped in cloth and holding an electric lamp and a vase of lilies. The well-used old leather sofa and easy chair have that comfortable look forever associated with apoplectic colonels exploding in their clubs over the latest outrage, as depicted in Bateman's cartoons in *Punch* during the 1930s.

This well-used farmhouse fireplace (below) might have belonged to a Thomas Hardy heroine, with the uncompromisingly large

stone flags surrounding it and a fire constantly, if not perpetually, glowing in the grate. Such a fireplace could be used for cooking or drying out damp clothes soaked by a downpour while out in the fields. One can equally well imagine a lamb being warmed and fed beside the baskets near the walk-in grate.

Apart from the Staffordshire dogs on the shelf, it is interesting to see the piece of crochet work pinned along it, adding a more domestic note to these practical surroundings. The way in which the lower half of the wall is painted a darker more serviceable colour than the upper half is also typical of what used to be common practice in larger cottages, domestic quarters and areas of the house associated with outside activities. The bottom half could then be cleaned or repainted, if necessary, before the upper, as it would receive more knocks or dirty marks. There was usually a painted line at the point where the two colours met, and the cream and pale green used here remained a popular colour combination from the 1880s to the 1950s. This example certainly contributes to that sense of the permanency and continuity of the traditional decoration which we expect to find in old English country dwellings and rooms.

CHAPTER FOUR

Taking Tea

*'Unlike most town teas, a country tea
should be rather a hearty affair. A mass of
sandwiches, preferably of at least two
types, a good sustaining cake and biscuits
are essential for gatherings of more than
two people.'*

As recently as twenty-five years ago it would have been possible to define England as the nation of tea drinkers. But changing tastes, mainly resulting from foreign travel, have brought the continental habit of coffee-drinking to England in a manner that fortunately has largely extinguished that gritty and bitter coffee peculiar to Britain. English second-hand shops

*A*lthough five-o'-clock *thé dansants* were once all the rage, there is little doubt that four o'clock is the generally accepted tea-time hour, still revered as such and left largely unmolested by the encroachment of coffee in the few remaining teashops, or hotels serving tea. In the country a hostess is expected to dispense tea to her guests from her best pot. There is still a certain feminine mystique attached to the taking of tea which survives from the early 'caddy days', when the lady of the house would open the tea-caddy and mix her own blend of tea before pouring in boiling water. Here, we see the modern equivalent of a ceremony that has lasted for over a century and a half. A silver salver holds a silver teapot of late eighteenth-century design with a milk jug on one side and a sugar bowl at hand. This is a serious tea party and not a casual affair judging by the number of knives and forks near the napkins, and the back-up supplies of hot water and milk jugs in the rear. Heart-shaped sandwiches, no less, stand beside a large bowl of cream, and there are ample supplies of scones, cream and jam – a calorific feast to be eased on its way with a torrent of hot refreshing tea. On a hot or cold day the clatter of tea-time cups and the buzz of conversation gladden the English heart.

Plants set on the sill before the leaded windows carry the countryside right into the room. Elegant sofas are filled with cushions of all shapes and sizes, and a small chair is covered

all seem to have a large selection of chromium-plated coffee percolators for sale. They now seem as antiquated as the British Rail tea urn and enamel teapot accompanied by thick white cups set on a perforated metal counter and filled with one swoop of the pot without stopping the flow from the spout, a procedure so memorably demonstrated by Joan Hickson in the film of Noël Coward's *Brief Encounter*.

Of course, tea-drinking in England dates from before the eighteenth century, but was then not as popular as the chocolate or coffee consumed in various 'Coffee Houses'. Stories of tea brewing where the leaves were eaten, while the water was thrown away, may well be true, but they hardly correspond to our image today of polite tea-drinking and the storage of the expensive leaves in tea-caddies provided with locks, so that the servants would not be tempted into the depravities of their betters.

Tea time, as we now understand it, gradually evolved into an afternoon meal from the late eighteenth century onwards, and attracted a number of domestic rituals with utensils for its celebration as the nineteenth century progressed. Many of these have vanished, including the appearance of the muffin-man on the street outside. Tea in the countryside, away from towns or larger villages, was naturally devoid of such a man, and as we know from Oscar Wilde's play *The Importance of Being Earnest* some people laid a great deal of store by what was or was not 'seen in the most fashionable houses' in the manner of tea-time food.

Unlike most town teas, a country tea should be rather a hearty affair. A mass of sandwiches – preferably of at least two types – a good sustaining cake and biscuits are essential for gatherings of more than two people. If there is to be a full tea party, alas, rather uncommon these days, then two types of tea should be offered – Indian with milk and China with lemon. To most of my 1950s generation, chocolate was considered something special; the mystique lingered after it ceased to be rationed, so a chocolate cake is always popular with China tea. There is also what used to be known as 'hospital tea'; Indian or Ceylon, which is stewed to a coppery colour, fortified with milk and sugar and served piping hot. It leaves a strange coating, probably of melted sugar, on the teeth and tongue, and is not recommended for polite tea parties. Some years ago in Japan I joined a group of curious ladies in a department store gazing at a moustachioed Indian as he performed his own tea ceremony. This involved boiling all the ingredients together in a saucepan, and the result tasted as metallic in flavour as the old-fashioned hospital tea. He did not sell many packets, but gained a round of polite applause, in admiration for such an audacious display.

with a bright modern fabric. A
nineteenth-century embroidered
Chinese hanging depicts birds in a
stylized setting and adds elegance to
the lime-green of the walls. Festoon
curtains are used as blinds, shading
the room from over-bright sunlight
when everyone settles down to the
serious business of tea and
conversation.

The traditional aspect of tea-time relaxation and jollity can well be appreciated in this comfortable setting where nothing much can have changed since the arrival of the easy chair some seventy or eighty years ago. Tea is laid on a butler's tray, resting on its folding stand. The lady of the house would formerly have been expected to dispense the tea, while the servants handed it round, together with the cakes and sandwiches which arrived with the appearance of the guests. Today, lack of servants means that everyone will hand round the food and assist the hostess with her tea party, which will no doubt be enlivened in chilly weather by a comfortingly hot fire blazing in the grate.

A more summery approach to tea is afforded by this glimpse of a delightfully informal setting for two, with sunlight streaming through the French doors onto the caned furniture, and flowers brightening the simple pottery on the table. The open door beckons the visitor out into the garden, surely the most enjoyable place for a truly English tea party, despite the insects.

*H*ere (right) tea for two is set in a palely restrained dining room that seems to have been devised for E.F.Benson's *Lucia* and its calculated mild manners. It was a widespread Victorian custom to have a family tea seated more functionally at a central table, without the fuss of small tables and the balancing of plates and cups that often accompany a drawing- or sitting-room tea. This arrangement has a dignified old oil-lamp converted to electricity, which will cast a welcoming glow over the food and the amusing monkey teapot. Again, the presence of a glowing fire will add to the comfort provided by the curves of the continental-looking dining chairs, and will bring the scene to life as much as the people who will soon enter the room.

*T*he charm of a fireside tea in
surroundings of comfort, can be
appreciated when looking at the
furnishings of this room and the
overall effect of the decoration.
Through the windows, framed by a
sumptuous display of red damask, we
can see the gardens. Gilt acanthus
leaves hold the curtains back from
the windows and the walls are
covered with a similar fabric.

Tea is laid out on a small tray in
front of the capacious upholstered
rosewood sofa covered with
buttercup-yellow damask, and a
leopard skin lends an exotic Elinor
Glin touch of the *femme fatale*, rather
at odds with the spirit of the spinet
and harpsichord. Family portraits on
the walls suggest a long line of
occupants who have imbued the
house with an established
atmosphere.

*H*ere is a cosy stove and a
farmhouse tea to induce that blissful
feeling of contentment that follows
the initial thawing out of one's face
after a frosty walk across fields as cast-
iron as the stove itself. Eggs fresh
from the farm are ready in their cups,
together with toast, all accompanied
by tea from the gaily decorated pink-
and-white tea service. The oak gate-
leg table has been waxed smooth by
generations of use and a bowl of
autumn apples scents the warm air. A
pot-plant adds a more sophisticated
note to this homely scene and the
Victorian hoop-back chairs beckon
the onlooker to sit at ease and seek
refreshment. Over the stove, a variety
of ornaments line the wooden shelf
beneath an engraved Christmas scene
showing a mail coach in deep snow-
drifts before a low, thatched cottage,
as snug-looking as this room is,
thanks to the heat of the stove.

There is a special pleasure attached to taking tea outside, especially on a summer's day, with the sun high in the sky and a garden full of flowers, trees and the sounds of summer. Whether as a picnic at a village cricket match or on the lawn of a country house, tea taken outside tastes even better and can certainly be made to last longer. For someone basking in a wicker chair in the shelter of this conservatory, a drowsy summer's day could be prolonged indefinitely, for tea is a leisurely meal to be begun and returned to at intervals, as one desires, while absorbing the delights of the room or the landscape.

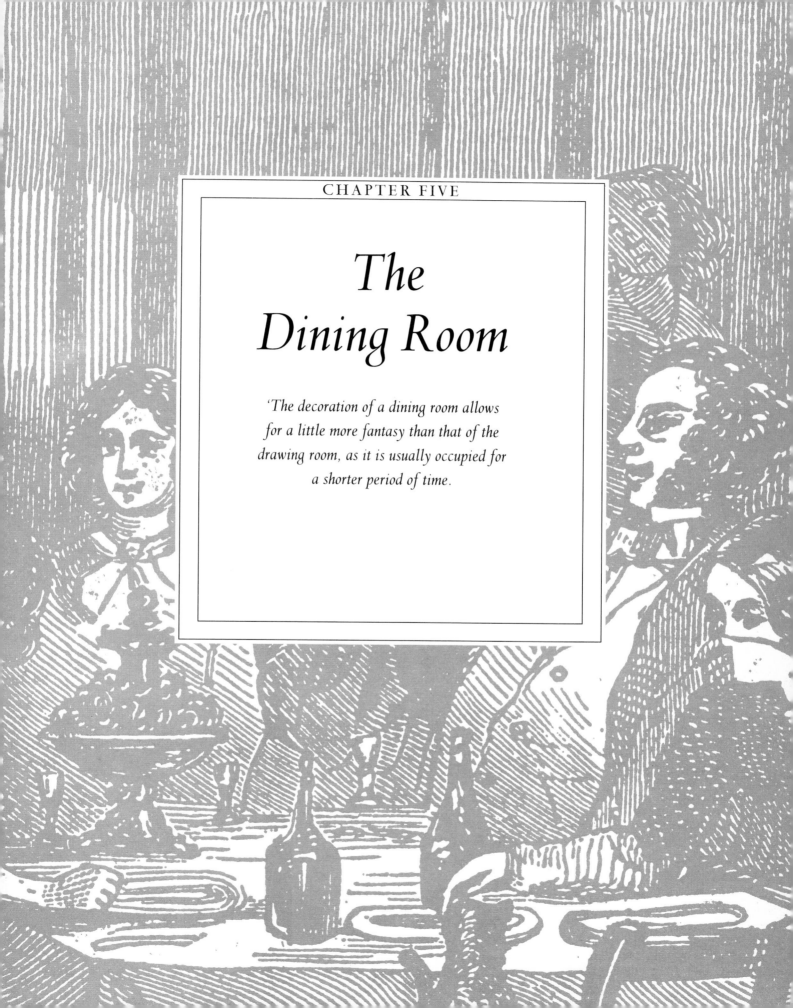

CHAPTER FIVE

The Dining Room

*'The decoration of a dining room allows
for a little more fantasy than that of the
drawing room, as it is usually occupied for
a shorter period of time.*

A dining room must be convivial, particularly in the country where guests may be at the table for some time, indulging their host's taste for large meals and quantities of drink. A gloomy or depressing room will suppress the merriest spirit, so it is essential that the decoration of the dining room receives as much consideration as the other rooms. It is not enough to fill it with a table and chairs and expect the rest of the room simply to happen as a matter of course.

Although a dining room will be used during the day and the decoration must be good enough to sustain lengthy scrutiny over a

long Sunday lunch, it is in the evening that its features need to be displayed to best effect. Dinner parties are generally far less formal today, but there should still be a sense of occasion about a dining room and it should have a seductive atmosphere by candle-light.

As with all the rooms in the house, there should be some reference to the surrounding countryside, no matter how small or grand the house may be. Atmosphere is important, but it must be pleasant and light, not overpoweringly historical with the room so crammed with family mementoes that the guest feels an intruder — unless the dinner is formal in the extreme. Soft candle-light on the table, warm lamplight from wall sconces and an open fire on chilly days should greet the visitor. The table should shimmer with glasses and be bright with flowers. If possible, fine silver ought to be laid at each place, and preferably on a shining white cloth rather than on small mats dotted around a plain, polished or dull, wood surface, however beautiful the timber. A cloth on the table lends itself better to festive displays of flowers and foliage than bare boards do, and a dining room should be a place of enjoyment and celebration.

The sad demise of table-cloths has deprived many a room of a sense of occasion and that special feeling of freshness, like having clean sheets. At one time, larger houses had linen rooms housing not only the sheets and pillow-cases, but also table linen of various types, and cloths of different sizes. Few people would probably now use cloths twenty-five feet long, but I remember them in my grandmother's linen closet complete with the date they were bought, some of them in her mother's day.

In the grandest of eighteenth-century country houses the dining rooms were indistinguishable, in terms of decoration and furniture, from those in the owner's town house, although in the largest country houses these were sometimes far superior in both taste and scale, once such a concept as a separate dining room had become an established feature of house design. We should remember that early Medieval houses of any consequence contained one large room or hall in which master, guest and certain servants would all eat and sit together. The Elizabethan period witnessed the spread of knowledge and culture generated by the Italian Renaissance, and in houses of reasonable size various living rooms were gradually set aside for eating in, away from the servants and other members of the household. The use of one room solely as a dining room was not generally established until well into the eighteenth century. Fixed dining tables were also developed at this time, to replace 'refectory' tables, which were folding or collapsible pieces of furniture, allowing the rooms to be used for sitting in or other forms of entertainment, according to mood or season.

*T*he carved oak sideboard or buffet of Jacobean design here complements the stout trestle table and the surrounding selection of eighteenth-century oak chairs. All the furniture has the mellow patina of age that blends well with the tiled floor and beams overhead, creating an atmosphere of continuity after generations of usage in what is clearly an old house.

Through the window can be seen the cold mists of winter, which the decorative panels arranged around the walls of the room, do their best to dispel. The table is laid for a hearty meal and draped with a cheerful tartan cloth. The low ceiling lends an intimate note to this country dining room illuminated by a fine array of candles casting a warm glow over the plates and glasses.

Candle-light also provides the main illumination above for a most elegant and inviting dinner table laid with a colourful cloth depicting sprays of roses, while a large basket of spring tulips fills the centre of the table. The soft blue-green colouring of the walls behind holds a series of panels painted with rococo scenes, and these are further illuminated by an up-lighter, which also picks out the lavish arrangement of mixed spring flowers on the stand in the corner.

The silver candlesticks on this circular dining table are complemented by a selection of military statuettes, with other silver ornaments and plates arranged with the rest of the tableware. The sienna-yellow colouring of the dado forms a contrasting background to the backs of the dining chairs, upholstered and covered in a gingham pattern of green, giving them a light and countrified look. That this is a formal setting is undeniable, yet the decorations of both the room and the table are maintained in an informally light manner, well suited to countrified rooms.

*I*t is difficult to imagine this oak-furnished dining room in a city house today. The solid quality of the oak table, chairs and cupboards is associated with traditional country houses of small size, as is the staircase leading up to the bedrooms, for this room is also used as the hall. We can see the open front door admitting a shaft of light into a rather sombre interior, enlivened in the centre by an arrangement of garden flowers.

Oak furniture has enjoyed various phases of popularity. In the early decades of the nineteenth century early oak furniture became popular, starting the first craze in the collection of English antique furniture. It was, inevitably, heavily faked, as the amount of genuine grand oak furniture to have survived nearly two centuries of use (or abuse) was, even then, small. As the century wore on and extensive church restoration occurred, genuinely old, carved or plain timbers became available.

Today the sale of antique oak furniture is limited; the 1960s and 1970s fashion for using it as the main feature of a modern room has faded for the time being. Yet the virtues of such furniture are obvious to those seeking to give either a characterless house or one older than, say, 1650 an air of age. The solid qualities of materials and design are well suited to country houses lived in by active country people. Once the door is closed, lamps lit and food placed on the table, a truly robust and comfortable atmosphere will be enjoyed.

Like the room in the last picture, this dining room (left) with its long trestle table evokes the countrified feeling of a farmhouse kitchen. The welcoming red-coloured walls contain niches filled with old English porcelain, and a restrained grey marble chimneypiece is embellished by a mirror on the wall flanked by a pair of hurricane-shaded 'lustres' (decorative glass table lights). The sophistication of the Regency-style dining chairs makes a curious contrast with the rustic simplicity of the table. A serving table and various pieces of primitive art add to this study in contrasts, all illuminated by bay windows, which can be covered by folding shutters at night.

The decoration of a dining room allows for a little more fantasy than that of the drawing room, as it is usually occupied for a shorter period of time. These two essays in 'countrification' (above and pp. 104–7) make use of *trompe-l'oeil* decoration in a different way, but both to good effect.

The urban version of a country dining room is the subject of continual experiment. This farmhouse-looking example (above) is to be contrasted with the genuine version pictured on page 98. The oak dresser contains a fairly sophisticated collection of china plates and dishes augmented by silver jugs and a couple of pottery tankards. The stripped-pine door is surrounded by simple, white walls that encompass the leaded window and its somewhat melancholy autumnal painted scene, fading away into a distant blue horizon. The table is covered with a beautiful white embroidered lace cloth on which are placed crystal glasses and crockery, illuminated by means of candles and a down-lighter in the ceiling. Two old country armchairs in the ladder-back style head the table flanked by wooden benches. This is a jolly, unpretentious room which achieves much by omitting unnecessary frills.

The last room had the cosy informality of a countrified kitchen, with a suggestion of an interior from the novels of D.H. Lawrence or Flora Thompson about it, in spite of the manorial quality of the balustrade painted in the mural. This room (pp. 104–7), however, achieves a much more cool and sophisticated look, part reality and part dream-world as evoked by the murals.

Murals are all very well in a large room, but they must be extremely well painted to survive in a small space. One way of ensuring their success is by using one of the many nineteenth-century French scenic wallpapers, which are still reproduced and easily obtainable. The likely effect can then be prejudged. The quality of the painting seen here (below and overleaf) is very high, but the lack of height in the room is obviously a slight problem. Such paintings, or the scenic wallpapers

echoed here, are meant to be placed above a dado-rail, so that the eye may absorb the details while the beholder is seated. The dado will then be left blank, panelled or discreetly decorated, because it is vital to have space for side-tables, spare chairs or other furnishings, which will otherwise obscure the mural and interfere with the desired effect.

In this instance the floor-to-ceiling painting is left virtually unencumbered by large pieces of furniture, but even the graceful Regency chairs and Empire table do detract from the overall impression. Nevertheless, the effect created – of a cool summer's evening – has considerable charm and will appear even more charming when the candles are lit and a dinner party is in progress, for candle-light will add to the feeling of fantasy that is part of the design and will lend a countrified touch to this city room.

The understatement of this country dining room echoes the form of decoration that emerged as a popular response to the English Arts and Crafts movement in the latter decades of the last century. The architectural feature of the arch is emphasized by white paint forming a contrast to the dark panelling of the walls and the light apple-green paintwork above. This method of colouring the walls and enlivening the darker panelling is no less satisfactory today than when first used centuries ago in English houses, and the Arts and Crafts re-working of a tested idiom has only faded in popularity within the last thirty years or so. Yet it is preferable to many of the strident effects attempted today.

The sitting room already discussed and illustrated on page 70 is in the same house as this dining room, yet no one would guess that either was to be found in the West Indies. The dining table, chairs, wine-cooler and objects on the table are so clearly English that the room might be found anywhere in England, overlooking a tranquil scene washed by rain instead of a landscape of tropical plants and foliage. But, as with the sitting room, this pleasantly understated form of decoration is as appropriate in these surroundings as back at home in England.

*T*he satisfyingly discreet gloom of stained panelling has here been blasted into the 1980s by pickling the stripped wood to form a busy-looking background for a circular dining table. The table has been laid with a cloth, enough candlesticks for a holy shrine, and a multitude of tableware betokening the coming feast. A sense of the antique is evoked, not only by the use of the panelling, but also by the bookcase used as a form of dresser to display colourful plates, a painting, and other objects. With all these objects on display, the curtain tassels and tie-back cords knotted around the upholstered reproduction open armchairs are a puzzling detail.

*E*ccentric details may be imposed on rooms by means of existing pieces of antique furniture, such as this delightfully monstrous example of that peculiarly English piece of dining-room furniture known as the sideboard. English furniture has always been noted for the functional qualities of many of its day-to-day pieces produced throughout the centuries. This sideboard has a functional use, but it is also decorative in the mid-nineteenth-century manner of creating both visual effects and an 'antique' atmosphere, as seen in Salvin's Thoresby Hall, mentioned above. The exuberant pattern quality of the design, seen in the carved frieze at the back and in the shape of the bases forming the pedestal supports, is heavily contradicted by the figures of the waving putti and the recumbent lions. There is a grotesque quality to the use of these baroque details, in conjunction with everything else, that suggests overfurnished Victorian houses and hints at Dickensian Christmas meals, when the sideboard would be groaning with meats and other fodder. This sideboard looks a little sad and lonely without the accompanying jollity of a hearty company enjoying succulent meals by the glow of a huge fire.

This sunny table, enjoying the views of trees and grass from the vantage point of a characteristically English bay window fitted with casement shutters, is anything but sad or lonely. A huge vase of flowers brings the summer garden into the room, the blue glass shimmering on the 1930s mirror-glass centre of the 'pool' table. Plants sit in an urn and a window-box is set against the windows. Neat little gilt chairs are placed around the old card-table, forming a pleasant spot for cards, writing letters or for a small lunch or dinner party. The informality of the setting can be dressed up by putting a cloth on the table and laying it ready for a meal, or the whole arrangement can be swept aside and turned into a complete sitting area, much in the manner of our ancestors, who liked to take meals in various rooms of the house, as the mood took them.

No mention of English dining rooms is complete without a reference to the English breakfast. Certainly the country dining room is the best setting for this calory- and cholesterol-laden meal. There is nothing more delicious on a cold morning than the smell of sizzling bacon, toast and coffee rising through the house, nor is there anything tastier than the mushrooms one has picked oneself, cooked and served on buttered toast.

Today, few houses will bedeck the sideboard in the morning with silver chafing dishes holding an assortment of fried eggs, scrambled eggs, bacon, sausages, fried tomatoes and mushrooms, all kept hot by spirit lamps or hot-plates. The days of devilled kidneys are dead and buried, as modern Englishmen reach for muesli or toast and marmalade. Coffee has supplanted tea in most houses, and the loss of the hearty breakfast has lessened some of the

enjoyment of the country dining room, even if we live to enjoy it for longer. Yet, how appropriate it would be to enjoy it in this semblance of a medieval Great Hall, the fire blazing and fire-light winking off the polished oak tables. Comfortably high-backed chairs surround the tables, and the light coming through the windows beckons one out to enjoy a ride or long walk in the fresh air and pleasant surroundings of the English countryside.

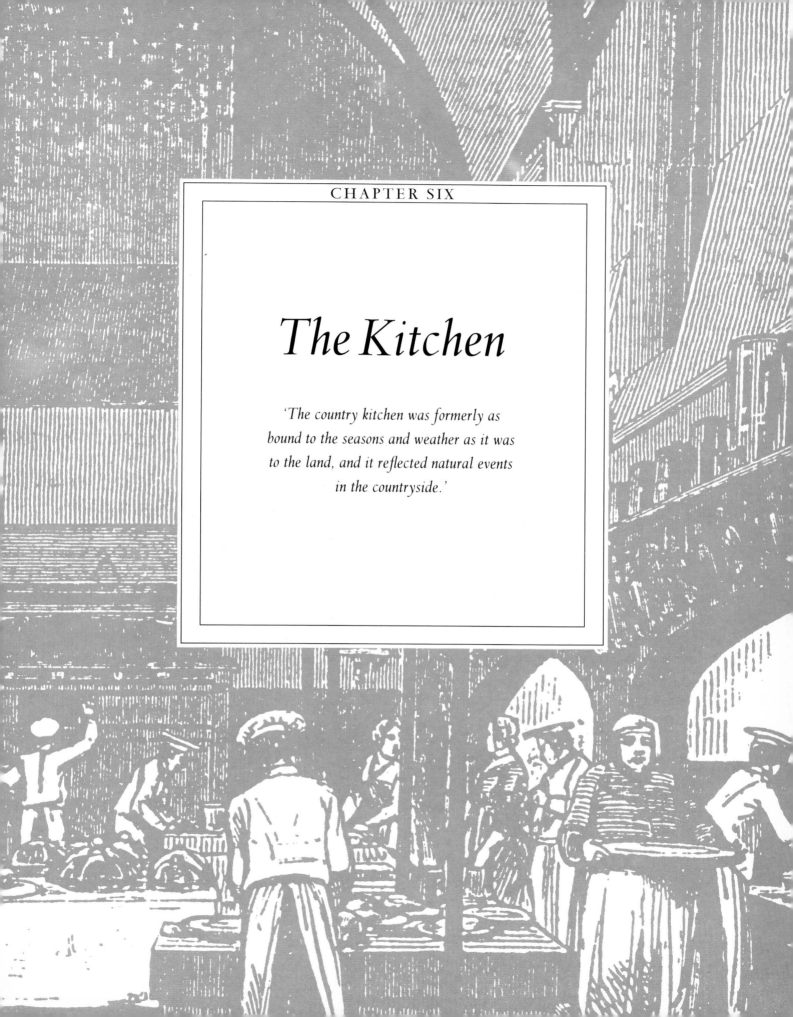

CHAPTER SIX

The Kitchen

*'The country kitchen was formerly as
bound to the seasons and weather as it was
to the land, and it reflected natural events
in the countryside.'*

*I*t is practically impossible to visualize an English house in the country without a kitchen, because everything in the surrounding landscape seems destined to end up there, and has done since the land was first cultivated and given some form of order by the colonizing Romans. No doubt Roman recipes survive, although no book has yet appeared to show how English country fare was transformed into the elegant Roman meals served in the villas scattered throughout England.

When I was a boy the remains of a Roman villa were excavated in the village nearby. While eating blackberries, my friends and I would speculate on the ingredients of their meals, as a mosaic pavement depicting fish was uncovered. We knew that fish had been popular many centuries later, because in the tangled undergrowth, choking the centre of a large tract of woodland in the grounds around my house, we discovered for ourselves the remains of a modest arrangement of fish ponds which formerly supplied the Hall. Also at the head of a lake in the grounds was a trout hatchery that had decayed and collapsed since the war, along with the boat-houses.

The English country kitchen with a well-scrubbed, serviceable table piled with the produce of the countryside: flowers, herbs, bread, vegetables, exotic fruits from the grocer and today's pet – or tomorrow's dinner?

Although bees were still kept in my infancy, pheasant rearing had ceased, but there were still plenty of pheasants around, along with the nests of free-range hens furtively built by the hens away from their designated place on the farm. Quite often the hens either forgot the nests or were driven away from them, and rodents raided the eggs. A large vegetable garden bordered by high eighteenth-century brick walls had supplied the Hall with all the produce it needed. The vegetable beds were set between pebbled paths flanked by low privet hedges, glass fruit-cases abounded, and a 'Mr McGregor' gate leading to woods was set in one wall, along the length of which pear trees were grown. So, with all this and the meat from the farms, this house, like thousands of others, had led an independent existence.

Today the countryside tends to be treated by those who do not live there as one large pleasure garden, not as a highly important place for food production. So much produce is now imported into Britain that it is easy to forget that the countryside used to provide nearly all our food until the introduction of refrigerated containers in the mid-nineteenth century made it possible to import antipodean meat and other foodstuffs.

Furthermore, in more leisurely times, and in most houses except for the very poorest, the preparation and serving of food was a more elaborate process than we are now accustomed to, involving several pairs of hands. In Flora Thompson's evocative reminiscences of country life a century ago, *Larkrise to Candleford*, she records how the majority of ordinary people lived and how they reacted to a tomato which then seemed extraordinary and exotic.

With the coming of the railways there was little out of reach for those with money to send for it, and the extensive use of cold-storage machinery meant the importation and distribution of more and more foreign produce, which did nothing to alleviate the apparently perpetual problems of the depressed agrarian section of Britain's economy. Today it comes as a shock to read in some novel of the 1920s that someone in a little country town could order a lobster, for fresh fish and other produce could easily be distributed on what was then an extensive railway network.

That elaborate culinary preparation lasted in England for a considerable time in both town and country is demonstrated by *The Ideal Cookery Book* by M. A. Fairclough (Lady Principal of the Gloucester Road School of Cookery, London, S.W.), which was printed in 1951 and contains 3157 recipes. As thick as a family bible this is clearly a reprint of an earlier success:

The mistress of the household will find this volume invaluable, as it states the time taken in the preparation and cooking of each dish, the average cost

Part of the change that has taken place in the country kitchen is epitomized in this view of an enormous fireplace, originally planned for that god of the kitchen, 'The Range'. We had a disused range at home, disused for cooking, which involved the operation of a multiplicity of cast-iron and bright steel doors, flaps and handles, but still in use until the late 1950s for the production of hot water in the kitchen – and it was boiling-hot water, with the unforgettable smell of hot copper as it burst out of the taps. The cat slept in the oven. Here, the range has been supplanted by its successor developed from an earlier prototype: 'The "Aga" anthracite-burning cooker designed in Sweden and now made in this country. It is noteworthy for its economy in fuel and saving of space.' This description is taken from Noel Carrington's *Design In The Home* published in 1933 by *Country Life*, which shows how the lack of servants was becoming a serious problem to be considered in the planning of suitable kitchens for new houses. (Judging by the kitchens, it is not surprising that something like the new art-deco Hoover factory in west London seemed a more attractive work-place for potential servants.)

incurred and when the dishes are seasonable. This will be found a great convenience, and will lessen the difficulty of ordering the daily meals. . . . The Editor wishes to draw attention to the large number of original recipes contained in this work; and, lastly, to the section of famous Viennese sweets supplied to her by Mrs. Fluss, of Vienna.

Apart from the elaborate construction of many of the recipes, involving delicious sauces or quantities of old-fashioned gelatine, it is interesting to see that certain things were impossible when out of season, now that we can buy almost anything all the year round. The country kitchen was formerly as bound to the seasons and weather as it was to the land, and it reflected natural events in the countryside. The section in Mrs Fairclough's book on preserves vividly illustrates this with recipes indicating 'Bottled Peas' or 'Preserved Siberian Crab Apples, Seasonable in September' (Recipe No. 3079). Incidentally, *'Topinambours À L'Italienne* (Jerusalem Artichokes, Italian Style)', Recipe No. 1465, had 'an average cost of 8d.' and was 'sufficient for 4 persons'. The illustrations are not far removed from those shown in Mrs Beeton's revised book of the early 1900s, with pictures of an enticing Yule Log, Tangerine Soufflé or, my favourite, 'Lawn Tennis Cake'. Plastered with icing the rectangular shape of this cake is sprinkled with 'very finely chopped pistachio nuts. Have ready a tennis-net, made of royal icing; set this on the cake, and place two tennis-rackets, also made of royal icing, at each side of the net. Average cost, 2s 6d. Time required, 4 hours.' Delicious!

That this huge volume should have been reprinted in 1951 reveals how kitchens had not dwindled to the mere stage-sets they often seem to be today, when people treat them as a combination of living room and dining room. The old way of treating a kitchen as a serious place of work for the production of well-balanced and innovative meals, irrespective of calories or cholesterol, has all but disappeared in the wake of convenience cooking, (justified) concern about diet or the demise of the kitchen help. What would Mrs Bridges have done without Ruby to scrub or chop for her? She could have hired another Ruby then, but not today.

The friendly appearance and warmth of the Aga is something of a magnet in country houses, and large kitchens often gradually become a sort of family living room that may also suck in the secretly unwilling guest, who had hoped to escape the intimacies of domestic life by going away for the weekend. Although there is an undeniable charm in the collection of multifarious objects set out on every available surface of this kitchen (left), the room is very personal in the way in which all manner of useless bits and pieces are kept in a certain amount of orderly chaos. It is not uninteresting, but it is as though the visitor has intruded into something as intimate as an upset bedroom.

One way around the problem of the extended use of the kitchen, when contemplating guests and not family, is to treat it as an extended farmhouse room mixed with a bit of nostalgia for vanished cooks. Thus, this most inviting room (above), with both Aga and open fire, has not merely a Windsor chair, suitable for the resting shepherd, but also a comfortably upholstered armchair in which any grumpy cook could take the weight off her feet. This kitchen is brought up to date by means of the colourful woven cloth hanging from the mantelshelf, in the style of the one of crochet work already seen in another country setting (p. 85).

*T*his nineteenth-century kitchen (seen in both photographs), set within an even older building, contains the traditionally stone-flagged floor, so cold to the feet when not given the occasional mat or rag-rug. Clearly it is a disused kitchen, and how sad the empty grate appears with memories of busier times, when the beams were slung with curing hams and pans gleaming in the light. Jam-making has been in progress; the fruit that was brought in the basket and weighed on the scales has now been cooked and put into the pots on the table. In Edith Olivier's very evocative book *Country Moods and Tenses* (1941) there are photographs of the art of 'Jam-Making Then' and 'Jam-Making Now', the latter showing a group of Women's Institute ladies chattering over their wartime task and pooled resources. As with a disused wartime aerodrome, this room still echoes to the sound of long-gone voices, the thump of the water pail and hiss of steam emanating from the long-departed cooking pots on the fire. At the other end of the room is the old stone sink with solid water-tap, an old-fashioned knife-polishing machine stands on the draining board and a huge door opens to the yard.

The farm-like charm of the foregoing illustrations is more poignant than this immaculately preserved section of a large country-house kitchen, with its glazed cabinet containing a gleaming array of moulds and cooking pots. The bells shown above are clearly those of a very luxurious establishment with no less than three billiard-rooms commanding the butler's attention. Elsewhere in the kitchen (right) is a well-polished dresser and a built-in cupboard, below the shelves holding more utensils. The bright copper surfaces are a friendly sight; indeed, everything is so clean and bright that it seems as though nothing has changed much for about a century; the very servants of the house at that time might stroll into the light of the huge window and begin work at any minute, so well preserved is every detail. The ghosts of cooks past must be well content wandering around this kitchen, where Mrs Beeton might just feel at home — although both cook and mistress would assuredly have their own recipes handed down through their families.

If entertaining in the kitchen is absolutely essential, then this interesting setting (left) is ideal. Apart from the large kitchen-table with the enormous marble top, the room is made interesting by the beautiful arrangement of the objects on the dresser, and a corner cupboard, here opened to reveal the useful sink hidden within. The size of this table was quite usual in old kitchens, one end normally used for the preparation of food and the other covered with a cloth, so that the kitchen servants could sit there, and even eat there if the whole table was not in use. However, such tables were usually made of deal with plain, scrubbed tops. This one has well-carved and polished legs with large brass castors, so was probably a dining or display table – if the marble top is original. Around it are a set of pretty nineteenth-century chairs of simple design, much copied by Morris & Company and named 'Sussex chairs' after an example supposedly unique in Sussex. The dresser also has a fine 1930s circular wireless set.

A dresser was once something of a standard fixture in most kitchens of any size. Apart from storing plates, usually of pewter in the early-sixteenth-century examples, cupboards might hold candlesticks, tinder boxes and other paraphernalia, while drawers were there for stuffing with much the same odds and ends we seem to accumulate today. Dresser bases in some areas had shallow drawers for candles, and the design of early dressers varied from one locality of England to the next. But these antique dressers are not usually seen in country kitchens today; their value has increased so much that only Victorian or Edwardian pine examples originally built into a specific space are more normally seen in a kitchen.

This stripped-pine dresser is still used much in the same way as when it was made, the bottom half containing mixing bowls and some baking-dishes. Today it also boasts a display of china and brass, which add to the decoration rather than form everyday objects of use.

*L*ike the last picture, this pantry is used much as it was when built towards the end of the last century. The typical red square tiles form the same cheerful and easily cleaned surface as when they were new, and the shelves house a variety of 'downstairs'-looking cups and saucers, with a selection of decanters above. This would make an excellent kitchen unit by itself, and would have formed a mini-kitchen as a Butler's Pantry, where glasses were stored, wine decanted and trays arranged. Silver might also have been cleaned here and tablecloths stored in the capacious drawers.

*T*hese two views of a 'country kitchen' (right), designed with great flair and humour in a town house, can be contrasted with a view of the same dining-room area on page 103. Here we see how the long narrow space filled with country furniture adjoins the kitchen area. The sophistication of this setting is apparent from the floor up. Large boards of hardwood give a spacious, warm look to the room, so different from the thin and worn pine examples with alarming gaps between them usually seen.

The table and dresser already discussed fill the dining area, while the cooking area is a clever combination of the old and new. An antique oak table in a recess holds an assembly of items, including an old hand-operated coffee mill, and these go well with the centrally placed modern version of an old kitchen table and with the ceiling rack above, from which a variety of both utilitarian and decorative cooking pots and kitchen implements are

hung. The convenient centre fitting not only contains useful cupboards but also shelves for large books. The marble top is most attractive and practical in this setting, revealing a feeling for the best of yesterday and today, and even the 'Olde Worlde' kitchen units are made to blend in.

Something of the urban
elegance of the last picture is also
present in this pleasantly decorated
kitchen overlooking clumps of
soothing greenery. Outside all is
rustic, natural chaos with branches
swaying and leaves whispering. Inside
there is an air of cool detachment.
White-painted walls and woodwork
are given warmth by the natural-
looking wooden surfaces and the
wood-block floor. The casement
window stands open, and light
bouncing off the leaded glass
illuminates the delicate Arts and
Crafts silver on the octagonal table.
The polished wooden centrepiece
reflects the colour of the flowers and
the Christopher Dresser pieces,
forming a distinct image of life in an

Arts and Crafts house of the 1880s. A cabinet with glazed doors against the wall looks as though it is by Mackintosh or Baillie Scott, yet chairs, kitchen sink and the accumulation of framed pictures on the walls bring us firmly into the 1980s without destroying the atmosphere of the past.

The wall cabinets, and the small window inserted above the worktop, are all details showing the evolution of this space into a room for country living. The room projects an image of a more recent, more suburbanized type of English country life in tune with the gardens of Gertrude Jekyll and the feeling of peace and leisure which forms so much a part of our vision of country life today.

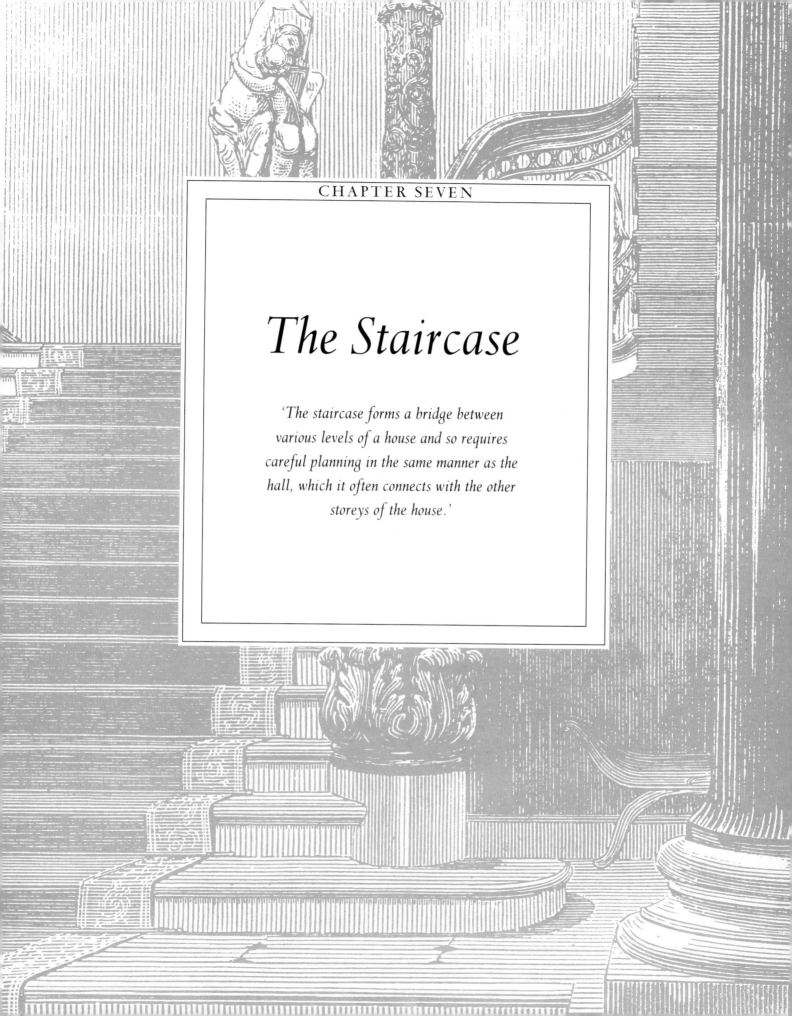

CHAPTER SEVEN

The Staircase

'The staircase forms a bridge between
various levels of a house and so requires
careful planning in the same manner as the
hall, which it often connects with the other
storeys of the house.'

The staircase forms a bridge between various levels of a house and so requires careful planning in the same manner as the hall, which it often connects with the other storeys of the house. To identify the two in a decorative plan is usual, but often mistaken, for although the two perform similar functions they do so in different ways. In all but the smallest houses it

The difficulty faced by those living in old English country houses can be gauged by this view of a broad tiled floor surrounded by stark white walls and leading directly to a very solid carved oak staircase. The decoration of the hall relies upon the architectural features of the door and staircase, which is linked to the hall by means of a continuation of the display of baskets filled with objects, such as hats or dried flowers, in what is clearly an evocation of an Elizabethan farmhouse. It is as though the farmer's wife will soon appear and take her baskets of farm produce to a nearby market. Through the open door can be seen an Elizabethan solid oak armchair and in the hall is a late seventeenth-century side chair. The decorative antique furniture is used to further the atmosphere, and up-lighters on the wall illuminate the ceiling, casting a subdued light over the scene.

is better to treat the two as separate units for the purposes of decoration. In doing so the decorator will also obey the older historical precepts of house design, although modern country houses will now be constructed so that hall and stairs form one unit.

This treatment of the two rooms as separate entities derives from medieval methods of house construction, when the hall first evolved as the nucleus of a larger, fortified, stone dwelling, in which the owner and his household both lived and took their meals. Rooms were added on, as some prosperity made itself felt, affording the owner and his family a measure of security and privacy. A staircase was later constructed, often outside the hall, leading to the rooms aloft, but sometimes inside the walls of larger buildings such as castles.

In *The Decoration of Houses* (1902) by Edith Wharton and Ogden Codman Jr a chapter is devoted to the virtues of a separate staircase contained within a separate space away from a vestibule or entrance hall. As that book draws mainly on the example of French eighteenth-century architecture, itself derived from Italian Renaissance examples, it is clear that the English treatment of the staircase evolved differently from its counterpart abroad. Of course, the development of Italian houses was fostered by the continued use of securely walled cities in which palatial buildings were planned without the fear of direct attack; fear of attack stunted the development of the English house for some three centuries. However, English walled cities existed; their inhabitants were just far less intellectually and culturally developed. Nevertheless, when the teaching of the Italian Renaissance filtered into France, the modelling of houses still relied upon a defensive structure for a considerable time and the same was true when the influences spread to England, so that architecture skipped several stages and contracted many ideas into a simplified setting. Wharton and Codman point out:

So early a writer as Isaac Ware . . . in his *Complete Body of Architecture*, published in 1756, continually speaks of the staircase as the hall. . . . Even after French architecture and house-planning had come into fashion in the eighteenth century, a house with a vestibule remained the rarest of exceptions in England. . . . Perhaps the best way of defining the English hall of this period is to say that it was really an Italian saloon, but that it was used as a vestibule and called a hall.

The point of this is to show that a staircase is usually a private route to bedrooms and should be kept separate from the public areas of a house by means of a vestibule. When Edith Wharton was writing, it was still possible to effect this in new buildings in America, but in overcrowded England we can only hope to make a distinction between hall and staircase by using different forms of decoration in both.

In smaller English houses in both country and town, it was not unusual to build the staircase into one end of a living room, a practice that continued well into Victorian days and undoubtedly began in the Middle Ages. A door to the stairs would resemble a cupboard door and, as above, open on to the steps simply rising up in a narrow space to the floor above. The door has been removed in this instance, so that light illuminates the stairs and creates a feeling of depth to a small hall with a tiny oak table and a few prints on the walls. A boldly patterned modern rug is a welcome touch in this potentially austere entrance hall and helps to bring out the colour of the wood. A tiny 'beehive' lantern hangs from the ceiling and adds a jaunty, countrified feeling to the area.

If the construction of the room permits it, then one solution to the gloom of many entrance halls in country cottages is to open up the space between stairs and hall by pulling out a wall (right). The timber construction of many houses makes this possible, although the effect may be less elegant than previously. In this hall the staircase is brought into great prominence by the architectural changes. Light floods the staircase and, combined with that in the hall, gives a bright daytime welcome with white walls and stained woodwork, yet the effect is muddled without a better stair-rail. The undistinguished angles and openings do not enhance the area, in spite of the functional bench and the useful caps and boots ready for action near the door. By night the effect will be better.

*T*his eighteenth-century pine staircase (left) has a mahogany rail and is typical of many thousands throughout England. It is eternally elegant and has been given a thoroughly countrified treatment by being stripped of paint in a manner never intended. Pine was almost always painted, as much to protect it from woodworm, as to beautify what was then considered a cheap and nasty timber. Colour was more important than grain.

At the foot of the stairs is a hall fitted with a practical doormat floor-covering on which a variety of plant troughs are placed; one is in front of a colossal Victorian mirror originally designed as an overmantel. This mirror reflects a show-case and a birdcage. Near the door stand the ever-ready necessities of English life: umbrellas in a pot. The stairs are clearly treated as part of the hall and vice versa, although there is interest in the use of paintings on the stairs and an unusual skeleton clock with a pendulum on the landing.

*U*pper landings are a kind of no man's land where the house is in limbo and the angle of stairs and the shape of the banisters can be made much of by the skilful use of paints and effects created by both natural daylight and electric light. All these facets have been carefully exploited in this early nineteenth-century setting.

The subtle curve of arches here leads the eye on towards light sources. Delicately turned banisters contrast with a heavy lump of oak furniture and a selection of small pewter tankards displayed around a large metal pot filled with flowers. Modern paintings give definite splodges of colour to the setting, as does the boldly geometric oriental carpet. A fragile-looking side chair makes a contrast with the other furnishings, but ties in with the banisters, lit by a stair-window and down-lighters. The muted yellow colouring of the walls is highlighted by white paint and forms a subtle background to an area full of pleasant angles and levels.

This staircase is most certainly treated as a room and is entered by means of a vestibule in the best architectural manner. A well-worn oak floor below is partially covered by a large Persian carpet with a pair of chairs and a stool in front of the chimneypiece. They merely nibble the edges of the carpet and so leave the pattern free to form a substantial part of the decoration.

The walls contain many oil paintings set upon differently treated wall surfaces. This early-eighteenth-century house is derived from Italian Palladian examples, and all the details of the architectural decoration visible here are adapted from Italian originals. Below the line of the stairs we can see a marbled treatment of the walls, again recalling Italian models, and the plasterwork, visible above the dado-rail near the large

Venetian window, forms a dividing line for this decoration and the pale green colouring of the walls above. The effect is, of course, very grand and very English in the way in which a potentially chilly-looking English room is transformed into a warm and colourful space. This is both atypical of smaller country houses in its urban look and yet typical of a time when large country houses were so full of family and servants that they formed small communities by themselves, a type of large village. We must also remember the distance from London of most such houses, and the fact that, although some families might have town houses for the season, many would remain in their country houses for long periods of time, hence the fashionably urban form of decoration, as it then was, in country houses.

One way of enlivening a dull staircase is by the use of a decorative stair-rail, or unusually beautiful banisters. In this house (the sitting and dining rooms of which have already been illustrated on pages 70 and 108 respectively) a necessarily shady hall in the house of an English family living in the West Indies has been given interest by means of an elaborate banister arrangement.

A Chinese Chippendale pattern of the mid-eighteenth century has been selected and adapted to form a most interesting play of light and shadow with its feeling for both English decoration and the exotic. Such staircases are rare in English houses, but the use of Chippendale's more playful style immediately reminds the observer of decorative furniture designed for the great houses of Badminton, in Avon, and Harewood, in West Yorkshire. There is also a hint of rustic outdoor decoration of the eighteenth century, suggesting those pagodas and intricate bridges placed in the more adventurous English country gardens of the mid-eighteenth century.

*I*t is most often the eighteenth-century houses of England to which the inhabitants of English houses look for inspiration and refreshment. The simplicity and lightness of design are continually more popular than any other period. The furniture of the eighteenth century and the houses are always in demand and always in fashion, no matter how they are treated or incorporated into antipathetic surroundings. The recent vogue for mid-Victorian upholstery and combinations of various patterns and colours is but a phase compared to the steady desire for well-proportioned light rooms and sympathetic colours.

The graceful design of this late eighteenth-century house is reflected in both the elegant staircase and the design of the fanlight set in the arch dividing the landing from the private entrance to rooms above. An early pianoforte is housed here and the space treated as a room; pictures, flowers and carpets are arranged in discreet order, and croquet mallets are ready for the fine weather which must assuredly shine on the fine green lawn set within a beautiful English garden.

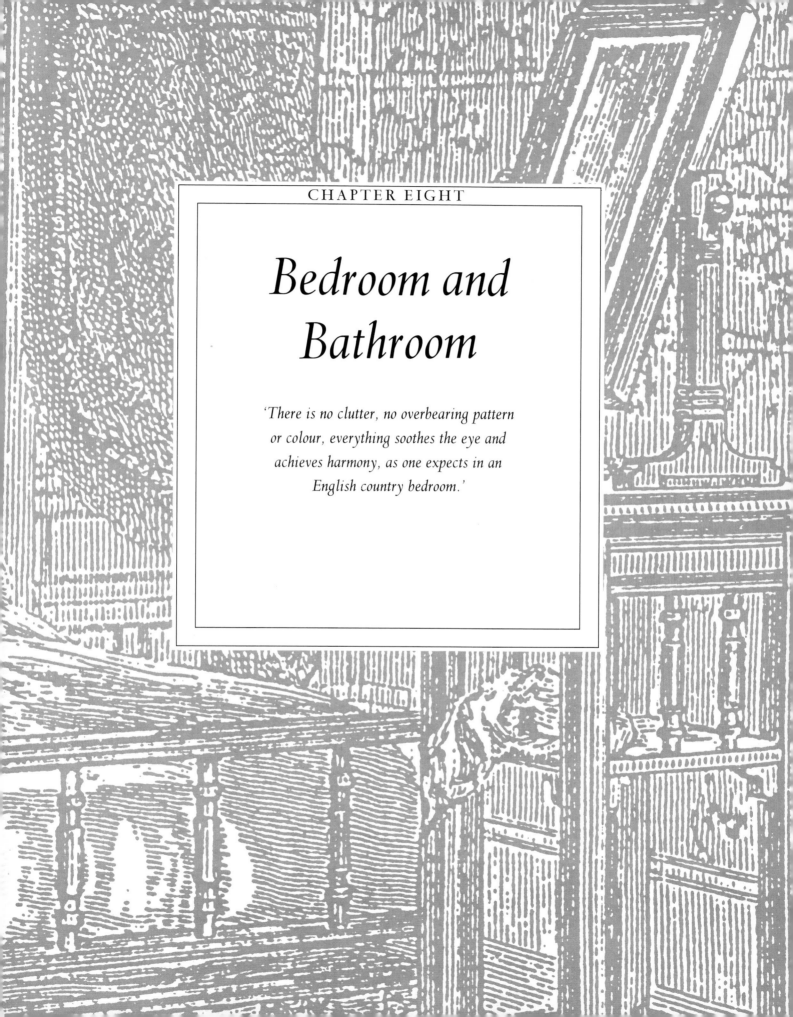

CHAPTER EIGHT

Bedroom and Bathroom

*'There is no clutter, no overbearing pattern
or colour, everything soothes the eye and
achieves harmony, as one expects in an
English country bedroom.'*

The Bedroom

As bedrooms are the most private of all the rooms in a house, it is fitting that they should be furnished in a most personal manner. Whether the owner wishes to reflect elements of the English countryside is a matter of taste. The grandest decoration has never drawn much distinction between decorative effects practised in town or country; if anything those in country houses have been even more lavish. However, the elements of fantasy or eccentricity incorporated in the owner's own bedroom should not necessarily lead him or her to inflict quirky effects upon an unsuspecting guest. For guests are an essential ingredient of a happy country-house weekend, however large or small the dwelling.

A country bedroom should therefore contain a comfortable bed, not a retired heap of springs salvaged from a relation's attic. A good bedside lamp and easy access to a bathroom are as essential as a welcoming atmosphere and, in winter, a draught-proof room. Irrespective of the contents of the decoration, these are the essentials of any normal guest-room and are notoriously neglected. A degree of shabbiness is no minus point as long as everything is well conceived, bright and inviting. Flowery chintz prints of sporting scenes or local views are always appreciated and add to the feeling of having escaped city grime and reached an interesting oasis. By the same token, a wall covered with someone's 1st XI photographs or similarly personal memorabilia is an overwhelmingly non-subtle way of reminding the guest that the room is only loaned.

*T*he above points were clearly in the mind of the original designer of this light, airy and spacious guest bedroom, which also has a useful luggage rack. The early Victorian furniture is as light as the pale lilac of the walls and the counterpanes of the inviting beds lying beneath the magnificent half-testers (canopies) hung with a dark green valance. The side curtains of the beds are modern chintz with a floral design in shades of green-blue, as are the curtains for the windows. A carefully placed *chaise-longue*, which is covered in the same fabric, offers a pre-lunch or pre-dinner moment of calm to look out at the countryside or read a book. The red- and off-white-patterned broadloom carpet is a soothing and cosy background to a comfortable room, as are the pictures and small ornaments on and around the chimneypiece, with its large fire-screen ready to hide the vacant black grate.

*T*his snug room set under a sloping, beamed roof forms a welcoming bedroom. Communicating with a larger room seen in the next picture, this one contains a tempting array of books and a well-upholstered Victorian armchair in which someone might settle down to read by the light of the lamp set on top of the stripped-pine print chest of drawers. Prints and a few well-chosen objects of interest are scattered around the room, which is provided with a white rug on the polished wooden boards. A cottagey atmosphere is also created by the patchwork quilt on the bed.

*A*djoining the room in the previous photograph, this bedroom also has a magnificent quilt spread across the bed. Apart from the architectural interest of the massive oak structural supports and beams, which writhe through the walls and ceilings, the quilt forms the main decorative feature of the room. Such features need only a little additional decoration, although the atmosphere of antiquity is underlined by the portraits on the walls, the quiet pieces of antique English furniture and other objects such as the 'zograscope' placed behind the chair on the left. This was a device using mirrors and a magnifying glass to examine the finer points of engraving methods.

*T*he late Felix Harbord was a master at creating modern interiors in the idiom of the past. Here at Luttrelstown he worked with his client, Mrs Aileen Plunket, to bring back to life a wistful-looking Anglo-Irish Gothic house. Apart from the welcoming fire in a simple chimneypiece, this bedroom breathes of the airy countryside, as Anglo-Irish in inspiration as its execution is English. The yellow-striped wallpaper is applied to walls without the benefit of dados or picture-rails. If a lower

bed had been used this wallpaper would have been a disaster. It would have accentuated the height of the room and further shrunk the small tables and chairs by the overpowering nature of its verticality. However, the mahogany four-poster pulls the scheme together, the compatible yellows of covers and hangings adding to the spring-like freshness of the room. A lesser talent might have been tempted to carry this luxurious look to its extreme, covering the floor in, say, white carpets, but Harbord

and client exercised self-control. In echoing a period, instead of slavishly copying it, there must be a balance between the past and the present in which neither one overwhelms the other, a basic concept in creating atmosphere in an otherwise sterile country room. As can be seen, a carpet of dark colour is covered with another woven with plant designs in faded colours. Everything is subordinated to the colours of the bed, even the pictures and objects on the chimneypiece.

A stark contrast is offered by this smart popular conception of a modern 'countrified' bedroom, which is far from restful with the busy pattern of the fabric covering a deep-buttoned headboard placed against an equally hectic, flowered wallpaper. Even the shades of the lights are covered with a patterned fabric matching the walls; nor does the circular table survive this onslaught of diverse patterns and colours in a small area. A picture in the corner is completely unrelated to the wallpaper, and a rug on the bed adds yet another unrelated design. Can the owner really relax here?

*T*his white-painted room, as soothing as a Swiss clinic after the previous bedroom, offers a measured impression of stability and calm. A somewhat spartan touch is given to the solid furnishings by the rush carpeting, but the strong shapes of the well-proportioned pieces of antique country furniture are an antidote. The modern lamps provide an up-to-date touch and are as strongly geometric in design as the bed and chest of drawers. A patchwork quilt also reflects a preoccupation with geometric shapes, as well as providing the necessary warm colours in an otherwise stark room. Apart from two small pictures, one of three cherubic faces, the room depends for its decoration on the harmonious blending of the furniture with the colours and textures of the floor- and bed-coverings. As with the Harbord bedroom (p. 147), the old and the new balance one another; there is no attempt at fakery or over-modern effects, so that any guest would feel welcome and at ease.

If a room is to be full of furniture, then it should be kept simple to enjoy the feeling of the country life to the full. This room is an open room, full of simple, pleasing objects. It is a room that looks out to the countryside for effects, remaining peaceful and offering a most enticing bed in which to dream. Pale colours expand a small room such as this and the light wood and hangings of the bed add to the effect. On the floor is a pale-grey carpet enlivened by an old oriental rug that visually links the eye to carpets on the landing and in the room beyond. On the walls are samplers, those early certificates of a girl's or a young woman's abilities with a needle. A snowy-white counterpane makes the room appear as fresh and clean as a snow-drift, while the rustic Windsor chairs set against the wall reinforce the country atmosphere of this quiet room.

*T*he kind of effect achieved in the last picture can be marred by overdressing a room in a variety of patterns and colours. In this quaintly shaped bedroom (left) the grey carpet is covered with oriental carpets, and a wicker chair adds to the lightness of the white paintwork. However, the pleasant Edwardian bed is so obviously made for a larger, more formal room that the room does not convey the same feeling as that illustrated in the previous picture. But as the most important piece of furniture in the room and one intended for more sophisticated surroundings, judging by its Maples appearance, it certainly appears as a comfortable centrepiece in an unaffected room. Two landscapes on the wall and the practical lighting balance the bureau bookcase in this comfortable country bedroom.

*T*he fashionable use of patterned wallpapers in bedrooms waxes and wanes, but the English have been great wallpaper enthusiasts for over two centuries. The use of an overall small pattern, as illustrated above, has gained in popularity, but needs careful handling. This example just works, in spite of the difficult angle of the ceiling. The small pattern is dark enough to form a background for a variety of paintings and a large double bed bearing a quilt with muted patchwork. An iron bedstead of a type popular throughout the second half of the nineteenth century is a solution to the problem of fitting the headboards of a large bed into a small space. The caned chair is, similarly, a good solution to the space problem. Though a personal room, it is neutral enough to house guests.

*T*his bedroom in the West Indies retains a feeling for England and its countryside. Today we are so used to the sight of cottagey white-painted walls that they no longer have any particular reference in our minds to either hospitals or the tropics. Because of the shutters and the bare floor we can guess that this is not in England, in spite of the four-poster bed with chintz hangings — also reflected in the cushions of the reclining chairs. A wash-stand and large *armoire* (cupboard) complete the furnishings of this room, but it is the Regency mahogany bed which hints at England in the days of the British empire.

*T*he most important piece of furniture in a bedroom is, after all, the bed itself. It should look inviting and, if it does not, then it must be comfortable. This particularly light version of a *lit bateau* (boat-shaped bed) has considerable charm and is enhanced by the hanging draped high above it, green on the outside and white on the inside, provided by a clean, cool-looking lining behind the head of the bed. An old, blue and off-white carpet gives the room a feeling of rolling fields and blue skies, something accentuated by the William Morris wallpaper and the glass curtains floating in the breeze. A cheerful patchwork quilt covers the bed and a warm fire burns in the grate, welcoming the inhabitant to the breakfast on the butler's tray.

Sophisticated decoration of English bedrooms has long existed, but re-creations of French examples only began towards the end of the nineteenth century. They were placed in London town houses and country houses alike, their popularity increasing during the Edwardian era, as Vita Sackville-West's novel *The Edwardians* illustrates. The large decorating establishments of Lenygons, Trollopes and White Allom were all accomplished in the creation of 'Louis' rooms, a taste that is still catered for today and has become an established part of the repertoire of English decorators.

In this Louis XVI bedroom for Mrs Plunket, Felix Harbord created a pastiche without the full treatment of imported *boiseries* (carved panelling) or French mouldings around the room, which his decorating predecessors used to install in their schemes. The chimneypiece and overmantel are the main elements of the room, giving recognition to the importance of architectural features. It is the vast Ritz-like double bed that carries a message of opulence, as the Edwardians would have understood it, in this 1950s arrangement. Yet, we can learn from it, as the colours could successfully be applied to a tiny room and create an intimate jewel-like effect. For this room is intimate, in spite of its large size. Apart from the bed, one large carpet covers the floor and a smaller carpet on top of that depicts sprays of flowers. A blazing fire warms the occupants, and a comfortable chair is conveniently at hand. There is no clutter, no overbearing pattern or colour, everything soothes the eye and achieves harmony, as one would expect in a proper English country bedroom.

The Bathroom

Only in the most recent country houses have bathrooms been something to boast about, unless one counts lavish inter-war examples – and they were relatively few in number. As recently as 1970, in his instructive book *David Hicks on Bathrooms*, the author wrote:

The bathroom is a functional room above all else, but it is also a private room, a room in which to perform certain rituals and in which to relax. It is an extremely important part of our environment. Yet, though we lavish the greatest care and ingenuity on making other rooms pleasing and comfortable, many of us tend to neglect the bathroom, and many beautiful houses are sadly marred by the drabness, unoriginality or plain discomfort of their bathing arrangements.

In the past eighteen years there have been great improvements in English bathroom decoration, but most will undoubtedly leave our foreign visitors politely shocked. Paul Cohen-Portheim remarked in his 1932 work, referred to above, that the English were the ones to affect the plumbing habits of Europeans in the nineteenth century, but the First World War marked the point of decline in that influence, as with so much else.

*W*here there is an empty room, a bathroom may be created. This was undoubtedly the original thinking when hip-baths became unfashionable. Very often the equipment of bath-tub, basin and lavatory were simply installed with yards of exposed snaking pipe and that was the end of it. Planning and room-conversions were largely for new houses or remodelled old ones. This pleasant eighteenth-century room was stripped bare and a serviceable tub installed so that the occupant might gaze out of the window and contemplate nature. A handy trolley holds neither cocktails nor medical equipment, but all the necessities of an indulgent bath. There is even a mirror in which to inspect the extent of the spare tyre. Wonderfully full green curtains frame the view and bring it into the room; a screen adds a useful draught-excluding and decorative touch.

*A*lthough bare boards in a room have a solid countrified look in the appropriate setting, there is no doubt that carpet provides the most luxurious touch in an ancient room such as this. The bizarre shape of the room means that the bath cannot comfortably stand against the wall or heads will be split by persons attempting to leave the bath. The bath is not enclosed, but is left to stand on its exposed feet protruding into the room, like the previous example. Many people find this look attractive and it is typical of the very early days of plumbing or even of later times when owners could not afford to or did not want to box in their tubs neatly. As a contrast, a luxuriously solid basin and stand are positioned under the window, and

the room is otherwise left bare and functional apart from a chair and laundry basket. This bathroom is in keeping with the decoration of the house, for it does not conflict with the atmosphere of age nor with the surrounding decoration.

*I*t is by the respect given to the atmosphere and age of a house that we judge its occupants, however unwittingly. It does not take much time to study a country house or to seek expert advice in order to know how to stress the good aspects of a house and thus form a sympathetic ambience. Nor does it take much time to ruin a country house by seeking to impose an antipathetic decorative scheme. Apart from the waste of time and money, the owner will never be fully at`ease, nor will he or she quite understand why.

There may be many solutions to decorative problems, but there is usually one perfect solution. For

instance, how many owners of an old country house, when faced with the problem of installing a guests' lavatory in a difficult space, would have thought of this solution to the placing of the basin? A delicately patterned porcelain basin has been set into a wooden top that is in keeping with the age of the tiny window in the sturdy wall. A pair of pre-war taps blend in with the setting, as does the tiny gilt-framed mirror. A collection of Coronation mugs adds variety and colour to the arrangement, a touch which is interesting without being over-personal, and the whole concept expresses the versatility of the best English country rooms.

Index

Numerals in bold indicate a major section or chapter, which include illustrations; those in italics refer to illustrations only.